Labor Pain

Just from My Heart Series

Chioma A. A. Menakaya

ISBN 978-1-0980-9858-2 (paperback)
ISBN 978-1-0980-9860-5 (hardcover)
ISBN 978-1-0980-9859-9 (digital)

Copyright © 2021 by Chioma A. A. Menakaya

All rights reserved. No part of this publication may be reproduced, distributed, or transmitted in any form or by any means, including photocopying, recording, or other electronic or mechanical methods without the prior written permission of the publisher. For permission requests, solicit the publisher via the address below.

Christian Faith Publishing, Inc.
832 Park Avenue
Meadville, PA 16335
www.christianfaithpublishing.com

Printed in the United States of America

I never dreamed I could ever
write! But now, here I am!
I write what I feel and
feel what I write!
My pen is my mind's feeling…
writing on my paper soul.

—Tribalman

To Odera, Chinagolum, and Dumebi,
who inspired this book.

May God give you heaven's dew and earth's richness—an abundance of grain and new wine. May nations serve you, and people bow down to you. May those who curse you be cursed and those who bless you be blessed.

—Genesis 27:27–29

CONTENTS

Foreword..11
Preface..15
Author's Note...23

Introduction: Are Children a Reward from
the Lord?...25
Chapter 1:   Mary, Did You Know?.......................35
Chapter 2:   More Tragic than Orderly..................44
Chapter 3:   It's a Paradox! 53
Chapter 4:   I Didn't Bargain for This! 63
Chapter 5:   Whose Child Is This Anyway?...........72
Chapter 6:   But with a Little Bit of Luck 79
Chapter 7:   It Takes a Village 88
Chapter 8:   It's a Misnomer!.................................98
Chapter 9:   It's a Conspiracy! 111
Chapter 10: A Critical Deception 121
Chapter 11: An Arrow in a Warrior's Hand........131

Chapter 12: Labor Pain: Personal Growth.............140
Chapter 13: The Travail: Spiritual Growth...........158
My Final Thoughts..175

Prayer for My Children 189
The Mysterious Dilemma of Firstborns 197
Prayer over Firstborn 201
Biblical References..205

FOREWORD

Few things in our diverse modern world cross the boundaries that separate us. One such phenomenon is motherhood.

The joys, fears, doubts, hurts, sacrifices, struggles, and, most importantly, a mother's love for her child are all universal. While each mother walks a separate journey, all mothers have a story to share. No one can understand exactly how much a mother loves her own child, but everyone understands a mother's love is deeper and more powerful than we can imagine until we take that journey ourselves.

Many mothers will agree that their child is an incredible gift from God. Until one holds their squirming, crying baby in their arms for the first time, they won't understand the immense new love they suddenly feel.

Some people wait years to become a parent, while others begin that journey at a young age. Some women struggle to conceive, while others seem to get pregnant easily. But God loves every mother and every child.

Most mothers feel inadequate as they face the prospect of raising and training children. We may not know what the road will be like as we raise our children; there will be difficult days, children will behave in ways we don't expect, and we will grow and learn along the way. Most mothers would agree they would never have accurately guessed what the road of motherhood would be, but there are rewards and listens along the way.

We might all walk different roads, have unique circumstances, or a creative approach to discipline; but as mothers, we share the universal idea of wanting the best for our children and doing the best we can with what we have. No two children are alike, and no two mothers are the same, but we can all embrace our gifts and love our unique children.

Join Chioma as she candidly shares her perspective and thoughts about the challenges, joys, and rewards of being a mother and what she has learned along the way. You will better understand how circumstances, culture, finances, religion, and upbringing can influence one's parenting style and choices in raising their children.

While we might feel inadequate to parent and oversee another human for several years, God equips us to be the parents He intended. Chioma doesn't just leave you hanging, wondering how you might accomplish such a feat. Instead, she points you to biblical examples to aid your path. She encourages you to stay the course as you invest in your child. Because, let's face it, along with the incredible joys and rewards, parenting can be a challenge.

Pam Lagomarsino, a mom

PREFACE

> The word of God is quick, and powerful, and sharper than any two edged sword, piercing even to the dividing asunder of soul and spirit, and of the joints and marrow, and is a discerner of the thoughts and intents of the heart.
>
> —Hebrews 4:12

The Just from My Heart is a series of thought-provoking books that came from my soul and will speak to your heart. This series is a presentation of my meditations as the *Qoheleth* birthed out of my reflection moments. I have an analytical mind, and I often lose myself in deep inner thoughts, which at times lead to prolonged pondering and periods of dialogue with God. These are my meditations, and most times, these meditations are my prayers, the sempiternal way I communicate with God.

Sometime in 2015, I decided to put some of my reflective moments into a series of books, each by the subject of my reflections.

As a deep thinker, I seek to learn the why of things or events, especially concerning relationships, love, hurts, failures, successes, and disappointments. Being a Christian, I often ponder on God's Word to understand his concept or gain insight into how they apply to each situation or perhaps uncover the lessons he intended. Those are my moments of sober reflections or, should I say, meditations. These reflections often become a mixture of the Bible, my cultural heritage and upbringing, and our current environment. My mind had mostly been a battlefield of all these elements mentioned.

In my ponderings, I seek revelations into God's perspective in the subject of my musings. Sometimes, I gain understanding and knowledge, and other times, I come up blank, confused, and could find no answer.

When I am enveloped in the overwhelming presence of God, I either write down my prayers, thoughts, and questions or vocalize them. In God's presence, I stay silent, praise and worship, pray, and question. I come to him with supplication, and I petition him, saying, like Job, *"Even today also my complaint is bitter [Lord]; my hand is heavy on account of my groaning [Lord]. Oh, that I knew where I might find him, that I might come even to his seat! I would lay my case before him and fill my mouth with arguments. I would know what he would answer me and understand what he would say to me. Would he contend with me in the greatness of his power? No, he would pay attention to me"* (Job 23:2–5). Like Jeremiah, I have been confrontational and said, *"You deceived me, Lord, and I was deceived"* (Jeremiah 20:7–13), pointing an accusing finger in between my prayer and self-pity hysteria.

If you have not yet figured it out, I mostly have a biblical reference to every situation in my life, a fact that I have been called out on so many times. Maybe it is because when I seek understanding or meditate, it centers on Bible verses and biblical stories. I also like Igbo proverbs, for they are full of wisdom, and I often use the few I know for analogy.

I ask lots of questions. Perhaps to me, to face life and situations realistically, I must ask questions. An Igbo proverb concurs that "one who asks questions will make it to his destination without getting lost." Therefore, I ask for directions and guidance.

As I seek clarity, a precise answer, a big epiphany, or as most will say, that great sign or handwriting on the wall, when answers are not forthcoming, or when I think God did not hear me or pay attention, or perhaps is upset with my questions, I lean on Isaiah 1:18. That verse is to remind him that he said it is okay that I come for us to reason together. Surely, Lord, you were not angry with Job and Jeremiah, I think, so you can't be angry with me.

I debate God and bargain with him. Honestly, as I am writing this, I realized that I don't always reason with him. How can I even reason with God? But I place my demands and expectations on him and then require him to bring them to fruition. I want him to see my reasoning for the answer I'm expecting from him, and I don't comprehend why he sometimes ignores my reasoning and rationalizations. When I bombard him with questions, most times, I either don't give him a chance to answer, or I was too preoccupied with my asking, or perhaps with sensing the right answers that I don't hear him when he does answer. I also call it foul when I don't like what I am receiving because it might require me relinquishing control, being humbled, or staying in the fire longer.

When my "wheeling and dealing" with God doesn't play out the way I want them to, I will move to Hebrews 4:16, *"Let us therefore come boldly to the throne of grace, that we may obtain mercy and find grace to help in time of need."* That might be my little surrender moment before the cycle starts again. God is too big for me to begin to comprehend or bargain with; I can't possibly hope to understand what God's thinking because his mind transcends mine. His understanding is unsearchable (Isaiah 40:28) and beyond measure (Psalm 147:5), yet I ask him questions and pray for answers.

My intention for the series is to provoke thoughts or perhaps guide someone else's curiosity; it is not to provide answers or conclusions. However, sharing my heart's cry and baring my explorative mind can help the reader handle, find meaning, or accept life's frustrations, mysteries, and uncertainties as they journey along with me. While the journey itself is significant, perhaps it may provoke the reader to look at situations or relationships with a broader view or perhaps build a community of people who struggle daily to find answers like me, especially within the Christian community. To my Christian readers, you are not alone in your questions, and it is okay to ask God questions.

God is God all by himself. He doesn't waste our experiences; God moves in mysterious ways, and his wonders he will perform, and his words never return to Him void. It must surely come to pass but in the way he intended.

Prayer

> Lord God, I am thankful that you are not against me asking the hard question. Help me see that your answers don't come verbally, they are vitally—in a deeper sense of your presence. (EDWJ 2019)

APPRECIATIONS

To the unction of the Holy Spirit.

AUTHOR'S NOTE

God Help Grammar!

A note to the reader about being grammatically correct. I will use some colloquialisms and idioms. At times, sentences will start with *because*, *and*, and *buts*. They will also be used in the context that may require *he* or *she*, and *man* for both male and female. *Gift*, *reward*, and *inheritance* will be used interchangeably.

This is done for immediacy and non-formality; therefore, to the purist, I beg your indulgence. *Mother*, *mom*, and *parent* will also be used interchangeably, and the first letter in satan and devil was intentionally uncapitalized. This is to be somewhat consistent in my writing and to help reflect my views better as the writer.

God Help Grammar!

Preacher D. L. Moody was lectured by a retired schoolteacher for this lapse of grammatical correctness (he uses split infinitives when preaching). His reply was, "Madam, when you see souls going to hell and grammar gets in the way, then God help grammar!" (Mick Brooks, EDWJ)

INTRODUCTION

Are Children a Reward from the Lord?

Children are a blessing and a gift from the Lord. Having a lot of children to take care of you in your old age is like a warrior with a lot of arrows. The more you have, the better off you will be, because they will protect you when your enemies attack with arguments.

—Psalm 127:3–5 (AMP)

I have started what would have been the first book of the series, which is yet to be completed. This book is the second in its series; it came about as a reflection of my meditations on children and parenting, especially my children and me as their mother. Motherhood for me has been a constant high and low and all types of emotions wrapped up together, and I often wonder what God thinks about my children and I and how he sees us.

More than pouring my heart, this book is my quest to seek understanding for just being a parent and then as a single mother who raised three kids. I also sought to understand my children, our dynamics, and parenting in general. The urge for this pursuit came from my lingering thoughts, meditations, and questions I table to God for answers or some explanations. It is part of my inner yearning to understand human relationships and the biblical perspective of my natural condition—a condition of persisting joy and pain, gratifications, and disappointments.

I have to juggle life like most parents, but unlike many, as a sole provider (spiritually, physically, and financially) to my children, I had to be their protector, guardian, succor, disciplinarian, confidant, counselor, teacher, and often, a punching bag.

From my point of view, I tried raising my children "right." Although challenging at times, being a single parent accorded me the sole opportunity to instill all the values I hold dear to me to my children unopposed. As a Christian, I did the necessary by dedicating them to God, exposing them to biblical principles, and surrounding them with my church family that poured into their lives as they were growing up. I tried to exemplify those principles and impress them in their hearts, according to Deuteronomy 11:19 and Deuteronomy 6:7. I raised my children in the way they should walk, holding on to Proverbs 22:6 that they will not depart from those values as they grow older.

I did what I know to do, to bring a balance to our lives and make them comfortable to the best of my abilities. However, some moments of rude awakenings challenged me further to ponder and dialogue with God (as I often do) in seeking understanding. It was my conniption fits, pulverized expectations, fears, shortcomings, and misgivings—as well as my joys, victories, laughter, and proud moments as a mother—that propelled my attempt at writing this book. It became a part of my journey to understand children and their roles and how they fit into human ecology.

In my carnal mind, I had expected that our lives (my children and I) be free of strife. After all, I am raising "first-class" children and expected that they should automatically "fall in line." However, that was far from the situation. So, I went on a quest for a good explanation that started in my thoughts. It grew to a persistent dialogue with God to provide what I considered a reasonable answer, especially for those hard and painful moments I experienced. I kept on with the tête-à-tête with God on the subject, which was really my boo-hoo moments and lamentations as a parent. My musings led me one day to Psalm 127:3–5; these Bible verses triggered more episodes of meditations, and they became my reference point for the answers I sought. I began to study them, meditating on them to uncover any deep meaning the texts may reveal, exploring the possibility that the answers I seek may be uncovered in those few verses. But it took me on a journey with many turns and rest stops that went beyond my children to other children I know personally, heard about, or read about. It took me to explore biblical children as well and motherhood.

As my thoughts grew, I needed to know more, to find out how everything relates as I dug deeper. I also wondered if there were others out there whose minds have thoughts such as mine. *Is there a mother out there who thinks like me?* I often wondered. *Does anyone battle similar thoughts like mine?* I often asked myself.

As I pondered on verse 3 of Psalm 127, I begged this question, if children are truly a reward from the Lord, how come they can, at times, be so much trouble? *You know! Those troublesome children*, I wondered. Those you sometimes wonder where they came from—the ones you sometimes wonder if they are truly yours, or perhaps if your child was switched at birth. What about children who sometimes exhibit behaviors that will make parents question where they went wrong as parents? How can we reconcile the fact that sometimes, our beloved children can be the cause of pain and sorrow? Yet, they bring so much joy and fulfillment. We desperately long to have them and love them dearly when we do.

LABOR PAIN

While thinking about children coming from Lord, it made sense to me that they should be a reward or heritage of good and not for evil; after all, "the blessing of the Lord makes rich and adds no sorrow" (Proverbs 10:22). If so, logical thinking then denotes that children, as gifts, should come sorrow free. That was going to be the premise of the entire book that I first titled with this rhetorical question; *Are Children Gifts from God?*

But God said, "Not so!" He had a lot to reveal on the subject as our dialogue continued. God is used to me rationalizing and analyzing as it is often my MO; however, it made me aware that I was making a *one-tail test* as my hypothesis is one-directional. Though it was a good starting point, I had not looked at the entire picture. Being one-directional meant either assigning God or my children with the burden of proof, and doing that will make me preliminarily the presumably right or the wronged party. That was also a call to look inward as I may not have been the *perfect mom* or a *first-class mom* or the epitome of what one looks like. Perhaps I thought I was. So, as I broadened my scope of exploration, I retitled the book; *Lessons from My Children*.

Verses 5 and 6 of Psalm 127 were hard for me to understand initially, and I made frequent stops there. When I considered the statement "blessed is the man, whose quiver is full of them," my mind went to an American reality television show, *19 Kids and Counting*. "Oh no! A bit too much," I must say, thinking out loud. Then I pondered on the following verse: "like an arrow in the hand of a warrior," and I wondered what that actually meant. My lack of a deeper understanding of those verses troubled me a lot. I was unable to clearly decipher their meaning or relate to them. I got stuck there often, and several times, I had abandoned my writing. Everyday stress and distresses of life did not help either. Before I knew it, days have turned into weeks, weeks into months, and months, in return, became years, until one Mother's Day, I heard a sermon that gingered me to keep on writing.

I am delighted that I have a finished book today, but its birth story did not end here. About a month after submitting my manuscript to my publishers and waiting to get their updates back, I had to change the title a second time. I made a few updates, including this addendum that followed.

July is my birth month, and I decided to join a church in a seven-day fast, starting on the first. Immediately, at the end of day one, as I emerged to break my fast, I got a shocker from one of my children. I have an adult child and two young adults at this stage in my life; so, I thought we have been through it all. On day three of my fast, I believe it was at about three in the morning, while on a live broadcast. I heard the words "labor pain." I knew I had to change the title of my book. In the days that followed, I began to receive some revelation into that title and had to make more touch-ups. One of such revelations was that if my book had been published earlier, it would be like giving birth to a preemie.

I ask that you journey with me as I try to decipher and put together my thoughts, experiences, and research in some worth-unmethodical way as they came to me.

This book is not a parenting guide. Therefore, this is not intended to educate, teach, and guide anyone on how to be a parent. My intent and prayers are that it reaches parents, especially mothers like me, who have battled with questions through the good and the not-so-good, the tantrums, joys, prodigals, and the emotional, the good child, the rebellious, and the conformers. I say to them, as my dad always told me, "Man's efforts at its best; the rest is up to God." I pray my book touches children too, to help them appreciate their parents more or extend grace to them for times they lacked understanding and did not get it right. Maybe it can help start a conversation and healing where there is hurt. To expectant mothers, I declare that the same anointing that opened the womb of Hannah be your lot, in the name of Jesus. Amen.

As a reminder, I am not writing to offer a solution or best practices for parenting. For starters, I am very unqualified. Second, I seek answers myself. And lastly, I hope that you, the reader, gain your own revelation as you journey through my book.

The Greatest Challenge in the World

My beloved brothers and sisters and friends, I ask for your faith and prayers this afternoon as I feel moved upon to discuss a subject which I have chosen to call the greatest challenge in the world. It has to do with the privilege and responsibility of being good parents. On this subject, there are about as many opinions as there are parents, yet there are few who claim to have all of the answers. I am certainly not one of them. I feel that there are more outstanding young men and women among our people at present than at any other moment in my lifetime. This presupposes that most of these fine young people have come from good homes and have committed caring parents. Even so, the most conscientious parents feel that they may have made some mistakes. One time, when I did a thoughtless thing, I remember my own mother exclaiming, "Where did I fail?" (James E. Faust)

Prayer

> Father, help me grasp that I don't need to know everything. When faced with difficult questions, may I accept that you will reveal to me all that I need to know, though not necessarily all that I want to know. In Jesus's name, I pray. Amen. (Selwyn Hughes)

CHAPTER 1

Mary, Did You Know?

Then Simeon blessed them and said to Mary, his mother: "This child is destined to cause the falling and rising of many in Israel, and to be a sign that will be spoken against. So that the thoughts of many hearts will be revealed. And a sword will pierce your own soul too."

—Luke 2:24–35 (NIV)

My first inclination was to try to understand or perhaps relate with the biblical moms and families, and what better place to start than with Mary, the mother of Jesus.

In the life of Jesus, who is the Messiah, though his birth and suffering were foretold, yet, his mother Mary knew no peace from his conception until his death. I pictured what my recollection of my first son's birth will be if I were Mary. It will be that of controversies, judgment, scandal, anxiety, and perhaps family feud. It will possibly be one full of anxieties, worries, fears, frustrations, and a few happy moments in between.

The motherhood journey started for Mary with an unsolicited pregnancy. I don't know about Mary, but if it were me, I thought, I will surely ask God the "why me" and the "why now" questions. I will ask him if I have to be his mother and if he can consider someone else, maybe someone older or with a little experience. I will plead a case for all the childless women I could think of. My plea will be something like this: "Okay, God, I know other Marys that are actually praying for children, just in case you missed that request. In fact, God," I will add, "oh, how they will praise you if you answer them. You see, it will be a win-win, for you, God, and them." I will plead my case and ask him to reconsider. Mary was in for it, from Jesus's conception, his youth, his persecution, his conviction, to his death; it brought a lot of heartaches, agonies, and pain to her. Mary's life, I presume, and that of her family and anyone connected to them will be forever altered.

"Behold, a virgin shall conceive, and bear a son, and shall call his name "Immanuel" (Isaiah 7:14). I wondered if Mary reflected on that scripture after the angel told her that she was the one chosen to carry the Messiah. She must have been familiar with that scripture from the Torah and never thought it would apply to her. What were her thoughts after her visitation? What did Mary think about the other scriptures that predicted her child's birth and the events that will follow? Was she jumpy any time these scriptures were read at the synagogue? What were her thoughts then? Did she have doubts or prayed that they would not come to pass? It must have been agony thinking about these prophecies, especially the one from Jeremiah about the killing of Rachel's children in Ramah (Jeremiah 31:15). What was it like in those days? Was it like today that some of us read the Bible but never thought it might relate to our present world or us personally? Perhaps it is just a story, a myth, or some sort of historical discovery.

I came across an interesting allegorical tale by author Dr. David Teitelbaum that may help bring a visual concept to the prophecies surrounding the birth of Jesus. And it goes like this:

> Imagine that in Waco, Texas, ancient scrolls are uncovered, which were written 600 to 1,000 years ago. Some were written before the discovery of America by Columbus, and all were written before the American Revolution. The scrolls predict that someone in our generation will be born who is of the direct lineage of George Washington. This person would be descended from

a long line of important founders of America, all of whom were known to be from Virginia. The scrolls further reveal that the person would be born in Tarrant County, Texas, in the town of Azle. Miraculously, his mother would be a virgin. At the time of his birth, dignitaries from other countries would mysteriously know about him and would come to worship him, and present him with precious gifts, believing he was a special envoy from God.

Dr. Teitelbaum also commented on how the rulers will try to murder the baby and how many other innocent children will also be murdered because of him, breaking their mothers' hearts. And this child will later lead a religious revolution when he grows up.

The Jesus story was a big saga. I love Christmas, and I look forward to the Christmas season as it is one of my joyous holidays. However, I do not think Mary will say the same if asked about her son's birthday, or perhaps she will answer with apprehension. Mary's life from the day of her visitation changed forever; her life became a soap opera. She was betrothed to Joseph, then found herself pregnant. Worst of all, Joseph was not responsible for her pregnancy. It must have left a big question mark for Joseph, and for him and Mary, a bad timing. *Couldn't this have happened after we got married?* They

LABOR PAIN

must have wished. If it had, it would have provided a good cover-up for us, especially for you, dear Mary. It seems that Mary was not so lucky with timing, for close to her baby's delivery, she had to embark on a long and uncomfortable trip from Nazareth to Bethlehem, the journey she made just at the nick of time for the delivery. The delivery itself was also not free from drama. In my mind, what followed should have triggered both prenatal and postnatal depression for most women, or worse, hypertension. Mary's labor and delivery ward was an animal shed. Their bad omen did not end there, but it was just gearing up. Immediately after the birth of Jesus, other babies were massacred on account of her newborn child.

These events must have brought too much guilt and confusion for any mother to bear. Then, amid their predicament, the angels appear to them, proclaiming that there is peace on earth. It must have sounded like a mockery to the young parents. Clearly, there was no peace.

With no time to ponder on what was going on around her and no time to recover from her postnatal blues, Mary, her husband, and the newborn Jesus had to take another journey. This time, fleeing to Egypt. They are now aliens and exiled in a strange land. All this just for having a baby! Mary's nightmares have now turned into a reality, and she must be hoping that these ordeals end soon and that her life will soon return to normal.

Poor Joseph didn't bargain for all this either. He did not sign up for all these dramas when he got engaged to Mary, and neither did Mary. Her distress that started from her baby's conception continued after labor and childbirth, and to top it all, her family is now fugitives.

As was told in the Bible, there were no dull moments for Mary and her family on her child's account. The saga and the rigmarole surrounding their child continued even after his crucifixion.

We must not lose sight that Mary was a mere mortal like us and feels like us. She was also very young, in her prime. God did not shield her from pain, anxiety, fear, and distress that came with her situation. Mary lived a mother's worst nightmare, and the natural consequences of being human no one would ever want to live. Certainly, a sword did pierce her soul. She knew struggles, disappointments, and of course, hardship. Mary also experienced defiance and rebellion from Jesus. Unfortunately, we did not know how much Joseph helped ease her pain and if he was supportive throughout their ordeal. Did he blame her and her son for all their calamities? Did their situation at times create a rift between them or threaten their union? We couldn't even begin to imagine how their relationship was.

At twelve years old, Jesus went AWOL while out of town attending a religious event with his family. When found, he seemed very nonchalant about the stress he put this family through. They couldn't understand this behavior or perhaps what provoked it. One could say that Jesus was defiant, disrespectful, and willful, and he even humiliated his parents. If we are conflicted about the behavior of Jesus, then we are in good company with Mary and Joseph.

Mary relived another nightmare, this time worse because it affected her child. She saw her son in pain and agony and was helpless to stop it. Mary witnessed his ridiculing, name-calling, mockery, and even being accused of operating under demonic influence. She was there as he faced the tribunal, on the road to Golgotha, and finally, her child's crucifixion and death. All these must have been too weighty for Mary, as it will be for any other mother (Matthew 1:18–25, Luke 2:1–7, Matthew 2:1–22, Luke 2:41–52, Luke 11:15).

There were many lows in Mary's life, but there were a few moments that I will consider to be some highs for her. Moments like the visits from the wise men, the miracle at the wedding in Canaan, stories of miracles performed by Jesus, his acts of kindness, the triumphant entry, and the respect he commands. Mary and Joseph could not be prouder of their son Jesus when he addressed the elders in the synagogues, as well as his command of the Torah. Yet, that same child brought them much distress.

The life of Mary's baby boy was far from the Christian celebrations of today. For her, Jesus's conception, birth, and death were no Christmas or Good Friday, yet he was the perfect child.

A Song in My Heart

Mary, did you know that your baby boy would one day walk on water? Mary, did you know that your baby boy would save our sons and daughters? Did you know that your baby boy has come to make you new? This child that you've delivered will soon deliver you

Mary, did you know that your baby boy will give sight to a blind man? Mary, did you know that your baby boy will calm a storm with his hand? Did you know that your baby boy has walked where angels trod? When you kiss your little baby, you kiss the face of God

Mary, did you know? Mary, did you know? Mary, did you know?

Mary, did you know? Mary, did you know? Mary, did you know?

The blind will see, the deaf will hear, the dead will live again

The lame will leap, the dumb will speak, the praises of the lamb

Mary, did you know that your baby boy is Lord of all creation?

Mary, did you know that your baby boy would one day rule the nations? Did you know that your baby boy is

LABOR PAIN

heaven's perfect lamb? That sleeping child you're holding is the great I am.

Mary, did you know? Mary, did you know? Mary, did you know?

Mary, did you know? Mary, did you know? Mary, did you know? Oh

Mary, did you know? (Buddy Greene/Mark Lowry)

CHAPTER 2

More Tragic than Orderly

> There can be no progress in the Christian life until we face the fact that life is more tragic than orderly.
>
> —Oswald Chambers
> twentieth-century Scottish
> Baptist evangelist

I believe that both Christian believers and nonbelievers alike can attest to the fact that conception is a mystery. In all of man's wisdom, it is evident that man cannot guarantee one a child. Yes, there are lots of breakthroughs in medicine, but science cannot guarantee conception. Divine intervention is needed.

A major challenge for women is barrenness; barrenness makes a woman feel incomplete (Genesis 11:30,

Genesis 25:21, Genesis 29:31, 1 Samuel 1:6–7, Judges 13:2–3, Luke 1:6–7).

In my culture, we regard children as the greatest blessing or accomplishment of a family, and there is a sense of shame and sorrow in households without children. As implied in the fifth verse of Psalm 127, the more, the merrier. Traditionally, large families are a blessing. The birth of a child is associated with pride, joy, celebration, and gratitude to God. It is the basis for what it means to be human as children bring a sense of continuity both for a family and the entire community.

These sentiments are seen in the Bible when Esau met his estranged twin brother Jacob and inquired about his entourage. He responded to him, "These were the children which God hath graciously given to me your servant" (Genesis 33:5).

Likewise, childlessness is associated with shame, a curse, and can be very painful for families to deal with. The pain of barrenness in the Bible is also apparent. Hannah, responding to Eli about her well-being, answered, "No, my Lord, I am a woman of sorrowful spirit…but have poured out my soul before the Lord… for out of the abundance of my complaint and grief I have spoken until now" (1 Samuel 1:15–16). Rachel, distressed over her childlessness, said to her husband Jacob, "Give me a child or I shall die" (Genesis 10:1). Childlessness can be very onerous on homes and marriages, while fruitfulness enlivens it. The book of Deuteronomy affirms that children are a gift from God and significant with prosperity. It is also a reward for obedience: "If you fully obey the Lord your God and carefully follow all his commands I give you today, the Lord your God will set you high above all the nations on earth. All these blessings will come on you and accompany you if you obey the Lord your God. The fruit of your womb will be blessed" (Deuteronomy 28:1, 2, and 4).

Fruitfulness was a promise of a blessing God gave his people Israel in Deuteronomy 7:14. He promised to bless them more than other nations as none of them will be childless. There are biblical accounts of women like Sarah, Elizabeth, Hannah, and Manoah's wife that God rewarded for their righteousness by turning their barrenness, blessing them with children after periods of infertility in keeping with his promise (Genesis 21, Luke 1, 1 Samuel 1, Judges 13).

Children bring joy, love, and a sense of accomplishment; while this is true most times, yet it is then ironic that both childlessness (curse) and fruitfulness (blessing) carry with it sadness, sorrow, heartbreak, anxiety, fear, and sometimes reproach. The Igbos often infer that those who have children sorrow over them, and those that don't, sorrow over not having. In other words, you are damned when you have children and equally damned when you don't. This saying speaks of the two different experiences, fruitfulness and barrenness, that share a similar emotion.

LABOR PAIN

A mother constantly worries over her children and is heartbroken when her child rebels or strays, yet nobody puts these emotions into consideration when desiring children. Most women feel unworthy or less of a woman if they are unable to conceive. I have once heard the agony of a barren woman as she pleads to God to allow her to experience pregnancy even if the pregnancy aborts. In her distress, all she cared about was the feeling that she could conceive. On the other hand, a woman that has experienced miscarriages thinks and prays differently. She prays for a viable pregnancy and might even cringe on hearing the infertile woman. Notwithstanding, people yearn for children.

Conception to most comes easy, and perhaps that ease may be taken for granted, while to others that are not so lucky, longing for a child can turn into a nightmare, as "hope deferred makes the heart sick" (Proverbs 13:12).

Whether by surprise (pleasant or unpleasant), the gift of children, planned or unplanned, is indeed a mystery and a creative miracle for which science cannot lay claims on. Man, in all their wisdom and scientific breakthroughs, has limited abilities in creating babies. Man can neither create nor recreate male and female seeds that produce children, nor can they fully comprehend the meeting of the two to form a fetus, nor the nurture that takes place inside a mother's womb. God is the Creator, and he created them "male and female, and he blessed them and called them man" (Genesis 5:2).

I thought of failed in-vitro fertilizations (IVFs), miscarriages, closed womb, stillbirth, and other childbirth tragedies and man's scientific reasons behind these painful experiences. I thought of the Ogbanje spirit in traditional Igbo society—an Ogbanje is an assumed spirit baby that is born as a human, whose goal is to torment his human mother by dying unexpectedly only to return as her next baby and then do it all over again. I also reflected on the ancient practice of twins' infanticide as they were believed to be evil babies. How does a mother go through such cruelty? I can't even imagine.

While still pondering over the joy and pain of children, my mind went to my cousin, who lost (all) her three children—toddlers—in a day in a car crash. What would have been better? I thought, would it have been better not to have given birth to them at all or to have had them for a very short time? I dared not vocalize that question. The more I consider all these different situations, the more I marvel at God, especially when man's reasoning is challenged. It is often difficult, especially for Christians, to accept the less attractive path of life, which is pain, hurts, disappointments, difficulties, and tragedies; they do occur and are, unfortunately, part and parcel of existing as humans.

Nonetheless, our comfort is that in the midst of these, God's mercies do show up alongside. God delivers those who trust him in their suffering; "he speaks to them in their afflictions," not from afflictions (Job 36:15). "Life happens." According to evangelist and writer Chambers, "Life is more tragic than orderly." Christians should consider this truth, commented another, who added that accepting this fact will help ease us from being "plagued by inner oughts and shoulds" that "leads down the road of illusion which results in frustration and anger. And though much about the world is still beautiful, accidents, calamities, and suffering prevail, and these will continue until the time when God brings all things to a conclusion."

A Flashback

> The hardest part about infertility is people telling you it's God's plan and then telling you to be patient.
>
> —Someecards

In my days working at the bank, I met a young lady desperately trying to conceive. She has spent almost all her savings on IVF, and her husband contributed some as well. She came into the bank to track the money her father was gifting her from his retirement money.

As fate would have it, I attended to her. As she laments her ordeal of how she had desperately tried to conceive, the monies she lost, and now her dad was going to chip in for her third IVF, I have heard enough, for holy anger came over me. I interrupted her as I got up and shut the door of my office.

I remembered holding her hand (she was looking at me with a strange look at this time), and I blurted out something like, "Are you a Christian? Do you believe in God?" I did not wait for an answer; I continued, "If you don't believe, I will believe for you. If you don't have faith, I will have faith for you." I was angry. I held her as I began to pray—don't ask me what I prayed because I cannot tell you what I said. The only thing I remembered was I kind of let out a subtle scream. I prayed, "Never, you will not lose money again over this. You will not lose your daddy's money, never." I could not remember how she left my office, and honestly, I wondered about that meeting for a while and forgot about it.

Fast-forward to about ten months later, I was attending to a client in my office one day, and I noticed that a lady was constantly peeping into my office to see if I was done with the client. At intervals, another person, more like a teen, will also come and peep in. Though they had a smile on their faces each time they sought me to notice them, I could sense their impatience. Their behaviors were odd to me as I do not know them, yet something was different.

This woman finally barged into my office as soon as the person I was attending to left. She marched without waiting for an invitation. In an overly excited yet calm voice, she asked, "Do you remember me?" With a smile, she added, "I see you don't remember." At that same time, the teen (I later found out was her stepdaughter) wheeled in a stroller with twins in them. She added, "You prayed for me." I was blown away: I was in awe.

How did this happen? I wondered. Something I did in the spur of the moment. I didn't even know what I was doing. I still marvel at that today.

Personal Experience

The age gap between my children was unplanned, and they came contrary to my expectations. I did not conceive nine months after my wedding, as was the expectation in my tradition, and when I did, it ended in an ectopic rupture. My first, Chukwudera, shortened to Odera (meaning that which God has predestined), was conceived less than two months following the ectopic burst. Almost everything about his conception was revealed to me. I told all the people that came to visit me at the hospital while recovering from surgery not to feel sorry for me or dampen my spirit—for I was in a very positive, happy, and carefree space through it all. I told them that the child I lost was not meant to be, but another is on the way. I was telling them about my beautiful baby boy Odera that will be conceived two months later. I must have sounded weird at the time; even hearing myself narrate his story repeatedly makes me wonder if I had kind of lost it then. Odera is also tired of me telling him this story repeatedly, especially when I want to reaffirm to him that the hand of God is upon him, that he is a child of destiny despite what goes on. I went on to have two other children. The second, Chinagolum (God is my advocate or God vouches for me), came five years later, followed by my daughter, Dumebi—short for Chukwudumebi (God walks with me or led by God). Chichi, as Chinagolum is fondly called, and Dumebi were also answers to my prayers, each with their unique stories.

What am I getting at with all these stories?

CHAPTER 3

It's a Paradox!

Every rose has its thorn. From a thorn comes a rose, and from a rose comes a thorn.

—common proverb

I thought about God, the Creator, and humans, the agents or channels that bring life into the world. I reflect on the testaments of childbirths that assert that children are divine gifts. My question then is, if so, why the pain? According to Proverbs 10:22, "the blessing [gift or reward] of the Lord makes rich, and he adds no sorrow with it." The gift of God is expected to be sorrow-free, shouldn't it? Why then is parenting very hard? Isn't it supposed to be all smooth sailing, rosy, orderly, and all proud moments?

The blessing of children brings joy, and as discussed in the previous chapter, people desire children and can go to lengths to have them, yet parenting is so daunting and not always so joyful. The paradox of the gift of children is best explained with these Igbo names that depict the joy and pain of children. On the one hand, you have names like Nwakaego—a child is better than wealth, and Nwabueze—a child is a king (the ultimate one can have), and on the other hand, Nwabuolu—a child is work or laborious. The latter makes me wonder about the gift or the reward of children. *Merriam-Webster* explained *gift* as "something voluntarily transferred by one person to another without compensation" and *reward* as "something that is given in return for a good or evil deed or received, offered or given for some service or attainment." In the case of a new life, God is the giver.

All gifts are neither a blessing nor pleasing to the beneficiary. Truth be told, at one point in our lives, we have not truly liked some gifts we have gotten, even from loved ones. On occasion, we have re-gifted them, passed them on to someone else, and thank heavens for gift receipts, we can also exchange them. Also, when we receive a gift from our foes or a suspicious gift, we have either trashed it or returned it. However, these situations do not apply to babies; we cannot re-gift (excluding adoptions), return, or dispose of them like material gifts.

I thought about gifts in the context of being a reward for good or evil (which can be in the form of a curse or karma), including rebellion, prodigal, defiance, and physically or psychologically challenged children. I also wondered what other parents like me think of children who sometimes push our proverbial last button or make us question the entire role we played in their lives or, better still, where we missed it as parents. Umm! I wondered what they thought of the "gift" then. I have also heard these utterances from parents: "I can't believe my child did that," "how can he?" or "I raised him right. He knows better or should know better." What about these popular sayings, I wondered, "terrible twos," "troublesome teens," or the exclamation, "Oh! They are just teenagers" or juvenile delinquents (also add adult delinquents to this list).

If the notion then is true that children are a reward for good and evil, with all these name-callings, I wondered which parent is the reason for their delinquent child or, better, the good one. *The good ones must be from the righteous parent*, I thought sarcastically. Also, I questioned who dared to put labels or judge children? We were once children ourselves, but as adults, we have sometimes made those judgments. Then a dialogue from my childhood days echoed, parents or adult telling defiant children, most times as a joke, that they hope they give birth to a child like them when they grow up (maybe as payback), or just for them to walk in their parents' shoes and experience what it is like to parent a child like them. Likewise, I had heard other adults tell children that they were behaving just like their parents when they were children. I have also heard it said of a child that he is "putting their parents through the same hell they put theirs." Yet children can bring a sense of pride to parents, hence these adoring Igbo names: Ugonna or Ugonnaya (a father's pride or trophy), Ifeoma (a thing of beauty), and Ezenwa or Ezenwata (a child king).

To connote either good or bad is the Igbo saying, "it is no surprise that a snake can only give birth to something long," kind of like "a chip of the old block" or "an apple doesn't fall far from the tree." These sayings have both positive and negative connotations and can be spoken as a criticism or a compliment that suggests that a child is just like his kin, especially his parents; this can be in terms of traits, physique, mannerisms, and the likes. I can hear my brother Kene's voice teasing and cynically asking me rhetorically where I think my daughter got her hardiness and willfulness from.

In communities, when a child's behavior is honorable, the adults will praise the child and attribute such behavior as exhibiting their communal traits. A good child is one that is hardworking, respectful to his parents and other elders, and kind. A good child is the one that does what he is supposed to do, the one that pleases his parents by obeying their biddings.

A child is flattered when he is good. He is said to act like "ibe anyi" (our kin). But when a child misbehaves, they are teased and said to behave like his other side of the family and not the one addressing the child. However, parental and communal traits have been used to explain behaviors. That is why in the traditional Igbo society, before people engage in a sacred relationship such as marriage, their families will go on a fact-finding mission. Igbos take pride in their names, families, and communities, and these are guided against polluting, especially through marriage. For example, to preserve a *noble* or *good* lineage or bloodline, a person from such a family will be forbidden to seek a spouse from a family known to have a penchant for stealing or a streak of insanity. And in some situations, they are also forbidden to intermarry from families known to have done some evil deeds, even when such acts were committed centuries ago by their forefathers. The traditional Igbo society practiced the biblical principle of "not being unequally yoked." Although these principles inform many jokes on whose traits a child exhibits, meaning, which parent the child takes after, like biblical warnings, they do have consequences when ignored. (I need to clarify that as Christians, we have the blood of Jesus for the remission of our sins.)

I thought about the word, reward, to understand children as a reward from God. That, too, goes both ways; rewards can be positive or negative. The book of Genesis gave an account of the stories of Abram and Noah. While Abram received a good reward from God, who made him great and turned his descendants into a great nation as a requite for his faith in him, the opposite was the case with Ham, Noah's son. Noah was displeased with his son Ham, and he cursed his son, Canaan. Thus, Noah declared that his grandson, Canaan, will be the "lowest of slaves" and a slave to his brethren.

In contrast, Noah blessed his other sons Shem and Japheth. In these stories, both the curse and the blessing were rewards. Noah rewarded his sons with evil and good for their conduct toward him. It is worth noting that Abraham is of the lineage of Shem, and later, Abraham's descendants became Israel (Genesis 12:2, Genesis 9:24–27).

So, does God give children as a reward for good and as well as for evil? If so, does God reward good people with good children and bad people with bad children? Do we now consider our standing with God as a prerequisite for the character of our children?

If the answer to the above questions is yes, it infers that parents and not children are bad. Good children, therefore, are from good parents and bad children from bad parents. I came across an anonymous poster that reads, "If there are no bad children, only children who act out bad because they have bad parents, then why are we punishing children who have bad parents?" Interesting, I must say. I have also heard it said that childhood characters come from God, but their environment influences their personalities. This statement was an explanation given for why some bad children came from good parents, and some good children came from bad parents.

James 1:17 states, "Every good and perfect gift comes from the Lord." I like the Message translation better, and it states, "Every desirable and beneficial gift comes out of heaven." Children are desirable and beneficial. *Beneficial* can mean rewarding, remunerative, and valuable. The Google dictionary describes *beneficial* as "favorable or advantageous; resulting in good."

So, why do we have difficult children? Who or what formed the traits they exhibit? Why did God reward us with the children we have? The gift of children, although sometimes very challenging, has helpful outcomes. There are lessons from the gift of children. As deduced from the interpretations of the adage "every rose has a thorn," it teaches that inherent in humans are imperfections, as the rose is beautiful and alluring, yet its prickly thorns do poke and are capable of piercing the flesh. Another interpretation teaches that something that begins as imperfect grows to become as beautiful as a rose.

We should also bear in mind that God "makes his sun rise on the just and the unjust, and sends rain on the righteous and the unrighteous" (Matthew 4:45). Conflict is part of man's essential nature and the essence of being human.

Your Children Are a Gift from God, Now What?

Maybe you've heard the phrase, Children are a gift from God. But we get tired as parents, and we can become a little frustrated with what sometimes seems to be slow progress in our children's lives. I love my children, but wow! Their behavior often stumps me, and sometimes I get reactive and lose perspective. I absolutely believe that my children are a gift from God, but sometimes God's gifts are hard work used to refine us. Just what does it mean that children are a gift from God, and how should it change how I parent? (graceandwondering.com)

Echoes

So you are a parent now! There is no turning back. You are faced with an awesome responsibility. Your job as a parent may seem daunting and overwhelming, and certainly frustrating, at times. The challenges are countless, but the rewards are measureless and worth it.

Did you receive a job description before deciding to accept the job? Did anyone tell you it would be easy? Probably not. But did anyone tell you it would be tough-tougher than you could ever imagine at times? No one told me. Oh, I know I gave my mother fits, even a near nervous breakdown off and on. However, I never experienced the problems and crises from her perspective. Then I had children of my own. What an eye-opener! The other side looks very different.

Of course, when we are children, we are never going to be like our parents. We are going to be more understanding and less strict or rigid. We are going to give our children more freedom and everything they want. That is what children think. And then they become parents. I remember clearly when I heard my mother coming out of me when my children were young. I was shocked and dismayed when I realized I was just like her. And then, all of a sudden, I began to understand her as a parent. (Sandie Kritenbrink, MSW, LCSW)

CHAPTER 4

I Didn't Bargain for This!

Making a decision to become a mother is momentous. It's to decide forever to make your heart go outside of your body.

—Author Elizabeth Stone

As fulfilling and rewarding as motherhood is, it comes with heartaches, with hilltops of joy and valleys of sorrow.

—Pastor Mark Newman
(GCC-Fulton)

Being a parent is tougher now than in my days as a child, I thought, but surely, the thrills, the ups, and the downs never changed. It remains one's source of the greatest joy and the cause of some of the deepest griefs.

Knowing all this, why then do we desire the gift of children? Why do we feel empty without kids? Why do we seek out the prodigals? Why don't we just give up and throw in the towel on the wandering wayward? What does it truly mean to have children? What are we seeking in our longing for children?

Sometimes the anguish associated with children starts at conception, especially in the past, when unplanned pregnancies carried a sense of shame or disappointment. The travail of a woman in labor is not a very palatable experience either. The anguish of labor also got attention in the Bible. The mother of Jabez must have had the worst labor pain ever that she made sure her experience went down in history by naming her child Pain or Sorrowful (1 Chronicles 4:9). Likewise, it was said that Rachel saw it fit to name her child Benoni, meaning "son of my pain," before she died from his birth. That name was later changed to Benjamin by Jacob, her husband, as the name Benoni was a constant reminder of how Rachel died (Genesis 35:16–18). I wondered what labor experience was at that time with no option of an epidural, labor induction, or cesarean birth.

However, for most mothers, labor pain precedes great joy. John 16:21 agrees: "A woman giving birth to a child has pain because her time has come, but when her baby is born, she forgets her pain because of her joy that a child is born into the world." To some mothers, their pain lingers even after their labor pain is gone due to the circumstances surrounding their conception. Even with the pain and sometimes the difficulties of childbearing, most women desire to be mothers but desirably at the right time and under the right circumstance.

Each life, irrespective of how it came to be, brings its challenges. From conception, a mother's life is forever altered. Her life, plans, schedules, sleep, aspirations, finances, resolve, etc., changes. For a long time, I tease my middle child, who challenges me the most that he put me through three days of painful labor at his birth, and he has not yet stopped.

A mother will try to the best of her ability to lay a good foundation of a moral upbringing, but at times, children, even those from Christian homes, become willful and tend to stray from the values instilled in them as kids. Those values were intended to help them navigate through life with lesser hardships and difficulties.

The willfulness of children was exemplified in Matthew 23:37, a metaphorical representation that described Israel's rebellion against God's protection, which provoked this lamentation from God: "How often I wanted to gather your children together, the way a hen gathers her chicks under her wings, and you were unwilling." I have often wondered when my children fail to see my heart for them, my intentions to help guide their path against unnecessary bumps on the road. Those are the times I question why children often choose to walk the more challenging path than take the opportunities extended to them for an easier route in navigating life. At times, they think it is unnecessary meddling, a control issue, or "because I say so" syndrome. I am amazed at times, and I just could not comprehend it. I have tried to reason or understand, yet I simply could not. My reasoning and rationalization all beg the same question: Why the preference for a roundabout and difficult path in life when easier alternatives are available?

Wait a minute! I paused. The children of Israel were serial offenders, suggesting that rebellion must be a human problem. One of the Christian clichés often used to bring hope to a mother with a wayward child is that "it took the children of Israel forty years instead of forty days to get to Canaan." The moral of the story is that by his good upbringing, that child will ultimately find his way back. To that, the Igbos will say, "No matter how long the termite has been flying, it will eventually [get tired] end up in the mouth of the frog." The adventure of the children of Israel as they wandered about for forty years in the wilderness is also symbolic of the biblical warning of the danger in dishonoring parents, which results in difficulty to a child (Exodus 20:12, Deuteronomy 5:16, Ephesians 6:2–3). The unquestionable irony to this warning is that, in reality, the consequence of disobedience tends to affect not just the child in question but their family as a unit and sometimes an entire village. As it is often said, "Ora na azu nwa," meaning it takes a community or village to raise a child. A rebellious or a wayward child does not bring shame, embarrassment, and dishonor only to himself but to his family and, at times, the entire community.

While I pondered on these facts, I also weighed in on some external factors that come into play, which make raising children harder today. Some children misbehave due to the negative impact their environment has on them and the wrong choice of friends. These often lead to behaviors that deviate. At times, I sympathize with my children with all that is going on in our world today; they are also torn between two cultures. As children from a Nigerian heritage in America, they are born into a family with different sets of principles (morally, ethically, and spiritually) than the environment they were raised in, coupled with the fact that they grew up in an era of a big cultural shift. It's then easy for them to be conflicted. Parenting is pretty much challenged in these "terrible last days," as was foretold in 2 Timothy 3:1–5. The Bible likens a mother as "a fruit-bearing vine" and children as "slips of olive trees" (Psalm 128:3). As with farming, unconducive conditions, be it soil, weather, etc., makes raising tender plants difficult. As millennials growing up in this new era where moral decadence is welcomed by the majority, hence the appellation "the new normal," and where discipline is now part of our history as an abusive practice, raising kids becomes difficult. It must have been difficult for my children to rationalize my rules and the different sets of rules outside our home. They see some of my ideologies and rules as archaic and sometimes harsh. Suffice to say, with this "new normal," Christian tenets have become unpopular. In such instances, my children and I are often deadlocked in our argument on some of our views; hence, we agree to disagree for peace sake.

Contending for the Christian faith now wears antagonistic labels that start with "anti" or end with "phobia." Our children, by indoctrination, compulsion, or otherwise sympathize with society due to these negative labels because we taught them kindness. As for the church, they have either embraced the new normal or chosen to remain mute, and for the most part, they play it safe to avoid being judged, persecuted, or ostracized. The Bible warns that we should not be misled, for "bad company corrupts good character." It reiterates that "rebellion is birth out of our association with many who are ignorant of God, therefore, called for a return to reasoning" (1 Corinthians 15:33–34). I believe that if this verse was written today, it might read like this, *"Evil and corrupt society corrupts and deceives our children, because the lack of morality is the new norm, and wickedness is on a rampage; therefore, our children have become oblivious to the truth."*

The Bible stands for discipline, including physical discipline; hence it states, "Spare the rod and spoil the child" (Proverbs 13:24). On many occasions, I have heard people who grew up in my culture attributed their hard work, success, and good morals to their mother's spankings and discipline. The purpose of biblical discipline, like in my culture, is to help build godly character. Those people have said that they strongly believe that they would not have succeeded but for their mother's tough love. But that was then. Today, all types of discipline are now categorized as abuse. Let's be clear that the Bible is not in support of abuse; hence, parents are warned not to exasperate their children to anger and discouragement but to bring them up in the discipline and instruction of the Lord (Ephesians 6:4, Colossians 3:21). I recalled a recent conversation with one of my sons about the joy it will give me to babysit his kids when the time comes. He replied that he would have to think about that as he does not want his kids spanked. To that, I responded that I do not wish to go to jail.

As an Igbo proverb says, "Nothing the eyes see will cause it to bleed." In other words, there is nothing new under the sun (Bible), but my eyes bleed with what I see today. Strange and unimaginable things are not only happening, but they have taken roots. Profanities and things frowned upon not long ago are now showcased everywhere, and no one is even batting an eyelid because they have become our new normal. Then I ask today, how does a mother compete with society? How can one protect their children? (You can't quarantine them.) How do parents avoid self-blame for the difficulties of their children? It's a challenge! It's a battlefield!

The Prodigal Song

>Henry loves the ballpark
>But lately, he ain't coming round
>Things have been so different
>Since his youngest boy left town
>
>Fighting seems so harmless
>Families sometimes disagree
>It's hard to know the reason
>Why he finally chose to leave
>But he's gone away
>
>And his father waits
>And he is watching, and he is hoping
>Though his eyes are weary, his arms are still open
>And his prayer, so softly spoken
>Please come home
>
>Now Henry sits and wonders
>In that front porch rocking chair
>Does his boy remember?
>All the love the family shared

And is he cold
Out there alone
And he is watching, and he is hoping
(Laura Story)

Reflection

A child, even one raised with great love and care and carefully taught, may choose, when an adult, not to follow those teachings for a variety of reasons. How should we react? We understand and respect the principle of agency (an agent owes the principal duties of loyalty, obedience, and reasonable care). We pray that life's experiences will help them regain their desire and ability to live the gospel. They are still our children, and we will love and care about them always. We do not lock the doors of our house nor the doors to our heart. (Bishop Robert D. Hales)

CHAPTER 5

Whose Child Is This Anyway?

> The monkey said that she can only defend the child in her womb because the one she is carrying on her back may have unknown to her plucked and ate a fruit from someone else's tree.
>
> —Igbo proverb

The above saying means that a mother may think that she has trained her child well but cannot always influence her child's behavior as the child might do something unexpected when she is not paying attention. When your child strays the right path and heads for a difficult direction or better, when he begins to exhibit character that is foreign to your home and his upbringing, as a mother, do you question what went wrong? When things are not going well, no matter how parents tend to rationalize the situation, they sometimes wallow in hopelessness and confusion, wondering like I often do if it had to be that difficult.

Do you blame influences from society, friends, or perhaps your family dynamics? Do you blame your parenting style and a whole bunch of other reasons? Do you think God has forsaken you or forsaken your children? These are a few of the questions I ask myself.

An African proverb states, "If a monkey holds her child in her arms, she puts handcuffs on him." To that, I ask, for how long? A mother should realize that she cannot always protect or influence her child's behavior, no matter her best effort on moral upbringing. Ha, this realization came to me as a rude awakening, and at some point, I had to learn to surrender to God, though not willingly but out of necessity. I was left with only two choices: worry myself sick or release it. I would often fret over what most would consider inconsequential, like not hearing back from my child after numerous unanswered calls from me or refusing to fall asleep late at night waiting for my child to come home. I had trouble surrendering as it became a repetitive circle of worrying, repenting, and contention with the child. This repetitive cycle made me wonder why Job did not leave things to chance but made atoning sacrifices for his children (Job 1:5). That question never leaves my mind. Why will Job keep doing this? There was no mention of rebellion, disobedience, or defiance about his children. We knew nothing of their character.

Job was said to be "blameless and upright" who feared God and shunned evil. I presume he must have run a godly household and raised his children right, yet he deemed it necessary to make atonement to God on their behalf. The Bible affirmed that each time his children will feast and party, Job will rise early in the morning afterward and would sacrifice a burnt offering for each of them, thinking, "Perhaps my children have sinned and cursed God in their hearts." It was said that Job engages in these rituals regularly. The Bible merely stated that his sacrifices were meant to be a preventative measure. Still, I do not know if Job acted on hunches or by observing some traits or habits in his children. Perhaps there was rebellion going on. I do not know. I wondered what Job knew that other parents didn't.

As I kept on digging deeper into a child's willfulness and rebellion, I became more aware of the characters I have often encountered in the Bible. Let's take a look at Absalom—King David's son, charismatic, handsome, Mr. Charming, daddy's favorite. He is described as the most handsome man in the kingdom. To crown it all, his name means father of peace or peace. I can sense that David had a lot of expectations of his boy that will later kill his older brother (you may think justifiably), he also sought of to kill his father, yet King David was a man after God's heart (2 Samuel 14:25, 2 Samuel 14–18, Acts 13:2). What about the abomination, or should I say atrocities of Jacob's sons, Simeon and Levi? In their guise to avenge the supposed violation of their sister, Dinah, they killed all the males in Shechem, the land they sojourned after fleeing from Lebanon. They captured their children, plundering their wealth and houses. Their actions did ultimately put their entire family in jeopardy.

We cannot talk about rebellious children without the sons of Eli. They were called evil and were regarded as scoundrels and said to have no regard for God, yet their father was the closest person to God at that time as the high priest. It is a big disappointment that Samuel's sons repeated the same sins as his mentor's sons and a shame that they did not learn from their fate. One would think that by observing firsthand, the behaviors of Eli's sons and their doom, which was the consequence, they would have made a better choice for themselves. How do we begin to explain the behavior of the daughters of Lot? Committing incest with their father! (Genesis 34:25–31, 1 Samuel 8:1–3, Genesis 19:30–37). The Bible has lots of stories about difficult children. Oddly, the story about Samuel's sons replicate Eli's, and I found no understanding in their stories or feel better. I found no comfort or assurance as no solution was provided for dealing with defiance in children. Do you know the things that stood out for me in all these stories? Rebellion in children is "ozulu ora onu," it does not exclude anyone, not even the children of the most dedicated parents, the noble, or those said to be the closest to God.

The parable of the prodigal son and that of the lost sheep (Luke 15:11–32, Matthew 18:12–14, Luke 15:3–7) were stories that denote acts of rebellion seen in children. It could then be argued that rebellion can be born out of foolishness, ignorance, or both. According to Maya Angelou, "When you know better, you do better," and an Igbo proverb begged the question: "What are we going to do with a child who puts on a loincloth and drinks from his mother's breast?" In the traditional Igbo society, a young child does not wear clothes (in those days, only men wear clothes—loincloths). A child can act out of ignorance because he thinks he's grown, but children lack life's experiences. So, when a child acts foolishly or is insubordinate, disappointing, or rebellious, parents are hurt and disappointed. These often show up unannounced and with no warning signs. Perhaps the recurrent stories of disappointing children of respected biblical persons were told as an alarm that rebellion is ancient and non-discriminatory. However, it is said that "one does not throw away their merchandise when the market is bad" (Igbo saying). Exemplified by the prodigal son's father, love and forgiveness propelled him to keep watch, praying for his son's return. The same made Mary and Joseph stay together through their ordeals and anxieties over Jesus. God himself also experienced a parent's heartbreak from the very beginning of man's creation, starting with rebellion in the Garden of Eden to his condemned son, then, us; yet, he still loves man. He was a good father to Adam and Eve, and despite the perfect environment with no worldly concerns, stresses, and distractions, as humans, they failed. What could their excuse be? There were no reasons or good justifications for their disobedience; they simply went against God's instruction. But, even in man's rebellion, it couldn't separate us from the love of God, our heavenly parent (Romans 8:38–39).

Denial or Incomprehensible

I stumbled upon Dr. Phil's show one day, and the topic was about children who are bullies. The topic centered on a fifteen-year-old boy trapped by four older boys (eighteen-year-olds) and had his butt tattooed with profanities, while they shot a BB gun at him, amid his protests and pleas to them to stop. The mother of one of the four bullies, the one whose son was said to have finished the job when the others could no longer continue their act, came out defending her son. Her thinking was that the actions described could never come from a child she raised; she could not make the connection. She could not wrap her head around the fact that her child could commit such evil, despite acknowledging that their acts were atrocious. Was she in denial?

A Thought

I don't think that this mother is alone in her denial as she could not envisage that her child will be capable of such an evil deed. It must be hard for a mother to comprehend such evil coming from her child.

The story about Samuel's sons in the Bible became a story of "lightning striking the same place twice," which will be an unusual occurrence. I emphasize my point with Samuel because of his status and since he had a precedent. Also, God personally picked him for ministry; he was a priest, prophet, judge and gained national stature as a seer. Why could he not see that his sons were unworthy to fill his shoes as his successors? Perhaps, I thought, he was in denial too, or they, being his children, he may have been the last to notice what was going on in his household. As it's said, it's easier to see the flaws in others than ours. This took me back to the earlier proverb about the monkey who said it will be difficult for her to defend her child's actions once the child is outside her womb. No wonder monkeys are said to be intelligent animals. I exhaled.

CHAPTER 6

But with a Little Bit of Luck

> The work of parenting is as challenging as every other occupation but far more emotionally intense.
>
> —The Theology of Work (TOW) Project

It is undeniable that most parents have struggled or are struggling with parenting. They have had their share of dealing with the challenges and heartbreak of a difficult child and the associated emotional exhaustion. Yet, parents are often blamed for a troubled child. Apart from God's grace, no one factor influences human behaviors or relationships, the parent-child relationship being one. As a result, they cannot be stereotyped. With parenting challenges, I have experienced judgments, whether intentionally or otherwise. I have been seen as overcompensating or too strict. With similar reasoning of being a single mom, some people felt I overcompensated my children to make up for their dad not being in their life. Others accused me of being too strict to defy stereotypes attached to kids raised by single parents. Besides, being too strict was also attributed to my being a Nigerian mom, as Nigerian parents are perceived as naturally too strict.

Conversely, when my children are doing well, I get kudos for a job well done by the same people that made the earlier judgment call. But I can't help but ask whether it was the overcompensating mom or the strict Nigerian mom that now got it right. Yes, I am not innocent myself in judging others, especially when my children were younger. I will often attribute bad behavior from children to a lack of home training—that is, parenting. Remember, mine was the ideal home, and I, the ideal parent (just being sarcastic). Once, a colleague of mine heard me brag on my children that certain behavior will never come from them nor be tolerated by me, cautioned that I had spoken prematurely. You see! "Unless the buttock is stung by a black ant, it will not learn wisdom" (Igbo adage). Simply put, "experience is the best teacher," and I learned not to throw stones.

Although we cannot stereotype parents too, culture does influence parenting style and a child's attitude. By experience, culture, culture clash, and cultural changes are militating factors on parenting and influencing a child's perceptions, reactions, and mannerisms. This is to say, sociological and social factors are mostly the broader influencers to a parent-child dynamic. Often, society is quick to associate a child's bad behavior or difficulties with divorce, trauma, and their likes. I have often wondered about this situation as I sometimes think about the effect of my divorce, tragedies, and single parenting on my children. I was a product of divorce myself but in a different culture than my children. My siblings and I stayed with our dad, and as the oldest, I played the mother role in our mom's absence. The village played significant roles in my life but not by the common interpretation of the word. Mine was mostly by association and observation. I emulated mothers I admire as I spent time in their homes. I made friends with them and brought home some of what I saw. Together with what I remembered from my mom, I was able to provide guardianship to my siblings.

While my children were growing up, although I had surrogates that poured into their lives and helped me with them, I often wondered how their dad's absence impacted them. Perhaps, I thought, some of their behaviors and frustrations were due to that void.

Having experienced both sides of divorce—as a divorcée and a product of divorce—one of the biggest differences I noticed was in adaptation. My children's experiences and mine, help expose cultural influences on how people perceive and adapt differently in similar circumstances. Children like me, raised in Nigeria, tend to absolve shocks (handle disappointments) and deal with life events better. It seems that we are inclined to have a more carefree outlook on situations like divorce or perhaps a more resilient core in our DNA. I never knew there was such a thing as a daddy or mommy issue until I lived in America. Although I learned about the Oedipus and Electra complex in psychology class in college, I thought it was all textbooks. Unlike my children, I was raised in a culture that rolls with the punches; parents don't discuss adult issues, seek children's opinions in such matters, or consider their feelings. Also, a child's norms and the way of life are usually as defined by their parents. Considering that in my culture growing up, divorce was very rare. Therapy and counseling were also a foreign concept, therefore non-existent. I lived most of my young life with a sense of shame from being from a broken home but masked it very well. Although I believe that in my culture, parents are genuinely unaware that their challenges and actions affect their children, parental situations; like divorce, polygamy, or multiple monogamous relationships are not considered "a thing." They are not regarded as consequential to a child's emotions, difficulties, deviant behaviors, or justification. Perhaps, though it is a fact that children do go through their emotional turmoil with a parent's difficult life challenges, they are suppressed or minimized due to indifference. Cultural dynamics and the significant presence of people around children may also help shield children like me from its impact and awareness.

I also reflected on the stereotype following children of single parents, especially single moms, as the most likely to become unsuccessful or engage in bad behaviors. That notion, I find to be rather fallacious. I had to challenge it once in a church meeting when a person misspoke in that regard. Sociocultural influences help to expose some of these misconceptions. If being a product of divorce or a single parent is blamed for delinquencies in children and other childhood difficulties, why then are those issues also prevalent in two-parent homes? I am yet to find an answer from divorce skeptics and researchers as two-parent homes offer no immunity to children's or parenting difficulties. Sociocultural elements and life events such as abuse, relocations, sibling rivalry, hardships, lack of parental guidance, parental lifestyles, disciplining or lack of discipline, method of punishment, smothering, exposures, entitlements, and a boatload of others, are contributors. However, an individual's experiences, feelings, and coping mechanisms can differ even with shared experiences and values.

This thought drew me to Pastor Rick Warren's acronym SHAPE, which stands for Spiritual gifts, Heart, Abilities, Personality, and Experiences. It's an analogy of individual characteristics inherent in people for service. However, it concurs and applies to the complexity of human relationships and behaviors, those intrinsic and external factors that help shape who we are as individuals. The commonality of rebellion in children is that it's prevalent in most homes, creeds, and cultures; however, children, like adults, are unique beings with their own idiosyncrasies. Also, considering factors like mental concerns and identity crises that often mask themselves as rebellion. Parents can at times misunderstand these issues for rebellion and are clueless on how to handle them when recognized. Because people tend to go for the familiar, what we deemed as rebellion might as well be a child in search of his own identity and not fit into a certain bubble. In other instances, the child may be dealing with psychological issues, peer pressure, or pressures from parental expectations. Thus, the rules of engagement with children are not a one size fits all or based on generalized expectations and labels.

An older retired professor friend of mine gave me an analogy by comparing children to fruits. As each fruit on the same tree grows, matures, and ripens at its own pace, so are children; if you pluck one prematurely or induce it to mature early, its quality is compromised, distorted, and will not be its best. Similarly, as the saying goes, no two snowflakes are alike. Although siblings may share some similarities, they have differences in their temperaments, strengths, weaknesses, likes, dislikes, etc. These differences sometimes lead to sibling rivalry and adaptive and reactive behaviors. Knowing this helps me in relating to each of my children. I also harbor some fears because of their unique temperaments and dispositions and the values I imbibed in them; those often make them vulnerable to the ills in our world. For example, I taught my children kindness, but they may be taken advantage of if their kindness is not applied with caution. Even when, as parents, we interact with our children in comparable ways in similar situations, the result from each child is often different as they perceive things differently. Therefore, it will be wrong to always categorize causes or look for who or what to blame for a child's wrong choices.

Parenting children is an honorable occupation; its effect most times is outside a parent's control. It requires a lot of prayers, knack, ingenuity, support, tons of grace, and good fortune. As Alfred Doolittle from the movie *My Fair Lady* sang, "A man was made to help support his children, which is the right and proper thing to do. A man was made to help support his children but with a little bit of luck." Agreed! Luck or good fortune is very much needed. No one is born into parenthood. As such, I believe parents grow and develop alongside their children. The way we interact with our children also changes with time, with each child, and at different stages of their lives. Ultimately, to be a parent, irrespective of the highs and lows, whether a child brings joy or disappointment, is with a little bit of luck—that is, divine providence. God's guidance and mercy are needed for both the parents and children.

The Uniqueness of Each Child

Every child is an individual, with special social, emotional, intellectual, and physical qualities. Children are unique. They are individuals, and no two children are alike: physically, emotionally, socially, and intellectually, each child is a unique individual. Because children are unique, even if there are common needs and characteristics that children of a particular age or stage of development share, they must be understood by their parents and teachers in their uniqueness, and their individuality must be respected.

For example, even in a single-grade classroom composed of 45 to 50 seven-year-olds, not all of the seven-year-olds will be reading at precisely the same ability level. They will also differ in the ways they are able to understand and solve word problems in mathematics. They will have different personalities—some will be shy, some will be confident, some outgoing, some quiet but competent. They will each have their own life experiences and feelings about themselves. They will have different likes and dislikes, interests, and needs.

However, this does not mean that a teacher has to prepare 45 or 50 different lesson plans, whether it is a single-grade or a multigame classroom. Instead, the teacher must be able to get to know and understand each of the children and prepare teaching/learning activities that will respond to and reflect these individual needs of children. As children work individually or independently, in small groups or as a whole group, they will each benefit in their own way from these activities. What is most important is that the teacher, who is primarily responsible for planning the daily activities through which the children will learn, should know every child and keep track of how well each child is able to learn. (unicef.org, Philippines' *Multigrade Teacher's Handbook*)

CHAPTER 7

It Takes a Village

> You know how they say it takes a village to raise a child? Just wondering if someone can give me directions to this village so I can drop off my kids.
>
> —ballmemes.com

Like in biblical times, children in the African traditional cultures are considered a thing of pride and a blessing from God for the whole community, thus a communal responsibility in raising them. Familiar are these African aphorisms, "One hand does not nurse a child" and the famous "It takes a village…" Thus, it invokes Igbo names like Nwaorah—everyone's child, Adaora—everyone's daughter, and Nwobodo—child of the whole town. These sayings and names express the viewpoints of the values of communal relationships and ownership that children represent. In my culture, not long ago, parenting was a shared responsibility. As such, it's easier on parents. Children run the risk of multiple punishments for disobedience and willful behaviors. They respect and greet their elders, including strangers, and dare not call elders by their first names as that was unthinkable. While a child may rarely get away with disrespecting his parents even in private (including being confrontational or talking back at them), they dare not show disrespect publicly. They also hope they are not reported to an elder—"the village"—for rudeness.

I thought about growing up in Nigeria as a young girl. At times, children were more afraid of their teachers or other relations than their parents. Parents also welcome the support and sometimes use it as a fear tactic by threatening a delinquent child that he will be reported or sent to the disciplinarian.

In those days, when you err in school, you know to expect a double punishment because your teachers will discipline you, and you hope it ends with the teacher. If you are unlucky and get reported to your parents, you run the risk of another punishment from them; the same happens if a parent also reports you to your teacher. The law of double jeopardy, as stipulated in the Fifth Amendment of the Constitution, does not apply, as you most likely get double (punishment) for your trouble (bad behavior). I thought of those days with a grin on my face. Other kids like you, will at times, chime in when they are not the ones caught in bad behavior. They will be quick to remind you that "you will be dead today" and will also threaten to be a tattletale to your parents or teacher. Your conduct is everyone's business, including your siblings and peers. I still reflect on those good old days with a smile. In my family, we do have people with job titles of disciplinarian and educators. Their homes are where family members send or threaten to send their children perceived to have fallen short of the family's creed. Part of a good upbringing in my broader family is education and respect. Bless their hearts, my mom and my godmother were one of those people; both earned the title of teaching children, especially girls, how to be prim and proper or speak "good English." I also heard about my auntie, Auntie Rachael, or Mama Ogidi as we fondly call her, who was said to have a way of bringing out the smart in a child. Her home was where you send family members to excel in school, and she did not disappoint. Uncles, aunties, and older cousins all played the big brother-sister roles; each home belonged to every family member, including friends and in-laws. I thought of how in our town, we were easily recognized as "the Menakayas," our family name, and most could not differentiate which parents any one of us belongs to.

Our extended family, "the village," which includes, at times, close family friends and in-laws, all share similar values. Our homes mirror each other's, and they were guided by biblical principles and the legacy of education, integrity, hard work, generosity, and oneness. Collectivism was very much prevalent in those days, both with rewards and discipline. I thought of how my children would have turned out if they were raised in a similar environment. My fears growing up were not so much about being punished, but how my behavior will affect my family, our reputation, or, worse, hurt the people I love, my family. These apprehensions helped put me in check and still do. I had to hold myself to certain standards, even when no one was watching. Unfortunately, most of these values are now perceived today as archaic, and rightly so in today's context. Today, except for a few instances like political reasons, everyone is mostly responsible for their actions, marches to the beat of their own drums, and is most likely held accountable for their deeds.

Proverbs 15:22 states, "Folly is bound up in the heart of a child, but the rod of discipline will drive it far away." Children typically are bound to do foolish and stupid things, and I was not immune from foolishness or youthful exuberance growing up. However, in my days as a kid, children do think twice before deciding to engage in foolishness as they hardly get away with bad behavior. Parents were parents, and elders were also parents and not so much their children's buddies nor dance to their dictates. Instructions came from adults, and they were to be obeyed and not debated upon. Bad behaviors were difficult to go unnoticed as, at every corner, the eagle eyes of the village were watching.

I thought of a controversial story I came across. It was about four security guards in Texas that flogged some children who broke into a shopping mall. When confronted by the children's parents that questioned their right to discipline their kids, their response was the following: "The village raises the children." The narrator of the story said, "Today, I reflected on this famous saying, 'It takes a village.' It is now just an ancient myth, even when you deceive yourself by believing it. I will ask you to try to discipline someone else's child in your so-called village and see how that ends up." I share a similar sentiment as the narrator. Although it is good for others to occasionally provide support to parents, I think the famous "it takes a village" quote is now quite overrated. In my opinion, the village can offer occasional assistance; however, parents should be raising their children and not the presumed village, not strangers, not the teachers, not the daycare providers, not the nannies and their likes.

I also recalled a TV drama I watched in the eighties in Nigeria. *The drama was about a boy whose mother doted on even though he was a hoodlum. His luck ran out one day, and he was caught stealing and was sentenced to be executed. He asked that his mother should come and say goodbye to him and be there to watch his execution. On his way to his death, he asked to speak with his mother. When she approached him, he asked that she lean closer so he could whisper to her. As she came close enough, he aimed for her ear and bit it off. The executioners and the crowd that had gathered to watch his execution were perplexed and questioned him. He answered that it was her punishment for not teaching him right from wrong. Had she done so, he uttered, "I will not be facing my death today."* Charity, they say, begins at home, and so does discipline, as an Igbo name demands—"omulu zuia," simply put, raise the child you gave birth to. However, some parents hide behind others to provide discipline to their children when they should be the first line of authority in their children's lives. Some cozy up to their children to be that "cool parent" that it becomes difficult for them to enforce discipline, while others choose to be nonchalant. The cool parent likes to be in their children's good graces, and most times, the children already run the homes, and do not even obey their parents. Nonetheless, some parents still acknowledge that it is their responsibility to lead and direct their children on how to behave, dress, comport themselves, their language usage, the company to keep, etc.; as well as, dole out and enforce discipline, not the village (1 Corinthians 15:33, 2 Corinthians 6:14–17, and 2 Corinthians 7:1).

While the churches drank the Kool-Aid, society has now redefined our new normal and dictates how we raise our children. Personally, withholding discipline in any form as a way out of the complexity of a parent-child relationship is like igniting a fire and expecting it not to burn. However, some parents want to do the right thing, yet it is undeniable that it has become extremely challenging today for parents to discipline children, and most are defeated. These parents are the ones who respect their children's personal spaces in their homes and pick up after them like the cool parent because it is easier to do than displease their children. Some pet peeves of mine are a dirty house and dirty dishes. I find it disrespectful when a child dumps their dirty dish in the sink and will not wash them, and worse, when they do, they just take care of their dishes, leaving the rest in the sink. You get my point! I had often wondered who they left it there for. Perhaps their imaginary maid. The defeatist attitude of parents may also be provoked by the fact that parents are inundated with their daily pursuits that they are exhausted and stressed. They would rather not deal with disciplining as ignoring seems less stressful while others hope institutions will parent for them. It's equally challenging to be that supermom, too, especially if you are a single parent; therefore, any assistance is a welcomed relief. But the village is now scarce, and when available, it's often risky to entrust one's child with others as values may differ.

As scripture reminds us, children should "learn first to show piety at home" (1 Timothy 5:4), affirming that the main responsibility of parenting ultimately lies with parents.

Say What? When Did It Become Someone Else's Responsibility to Raise My Kids?

I see parents—I am one of those parents—who want to drop off and tune out, who assume that as long as their child is getting shuttled to school, youth group, to dance class and gymnastics and swimming and baseball and football and summer camp and Sunday school and preschool and daycare and afterschool programs, they are getting what they need. They are being instructed, and that's enough.

And then we all come home, finally, after a day of being shuttled from one certified instructor to another, and we let technology take over. Television, computers, video games, tablets, & cell phones take the place of engagement. Worse yet, the content of these devices is barely monitored. We throw up our hands. What can we do? It's just what's out there. That's just the way things are these days.

My issue is not with the teachers, but with this growing societal notion that sending our kids to school or Sunday school or any other number of structured activities somehow lets parents off the hook. Even the best teacher cannot give a child the true Biblical instruction and discipline that comes only from a God-fearing parent. And frankly, a lack of instruction and discipline at home makes those hard-working teachers become even less effective. What a vicious cycle. (Ruth Soukup, "Why We Won't Let a Village Raise Our Kids")

97

CHAPTER 8

It's a Misnomer!

> If you have never been hated by your child, you have never been a parent.
>
> —Bette Davis

According to popular opinions, correcting children and making them do chores is now perceived as abusive and traumatizing. For parents, it becomes difficult to correct children and also teach them responsibility and respect. Most parents now circumvent training or discipline to be safe from societal condemnation and their children's bitterness.

Evangelist Billy Graham warned that "a child who is allowed to be disrespectful to his parents will not have true respect for anyone." Yet most child experts today, including Christian psychologists, are toeing the line that the good-old parenting is abusive and creates "potential psychological dangers and emotional hazards." Their focus is on building a child's ego. Author John MacArthur condemns this idea as "dispensing anti-biblical advice." He states that the consequence of protecting the so-called child's esteem obstructs the development of a child's problem-solving skills.

These experts now have a new label for parents, "toxic parents." They claim that parents do unloving things like discipline, fear tactics, obligation, or guilt in the name of loving their child.

I find this fancy concept to be balderdash. It is built on blames, excuses, and generalizations and does more harm than good. It is divisive, and it does not seek a path to harmony. It also sabotages parenting efforts and provides an excuse that helps widen the discord between parents and children by creating or encouraging resentment and antipathy toward parents. These experts gave life to their theory by making it a diagnosed condition and a justification for children to hold their parents accountable for their shortcomings rather than seek a way to reconciliation, thus creating a new culture of contempt for parents.

Blame comes when a child is having difficulties, but no theory is coined when a disciplined child thrives. As an Igbo saying goes, "Everybody loves a fool, but nobody wants him for a son." Children need skills to enable them to function as adults as well as learn respect—respect for God, self, authorities, others, property, and responsibilities. Unlike in the culture I grew up, I observed that children now are clueless about asking for forgiveness, pleading for mercy, or saying thank you. I remember in those days when you don't wait for your parents to finish pronouncing your punishment before you begin pleading for their mercy. This is a strategy on a child's part to soften their parent's heart or the adult doling out the punishment. Also, no matter how painful the punishment, you are quick to add a thank you when completed, an act that shows remorse and respect for authority. Not saying thanks when released from punishment will likely earn you another round.

Parents have the responsibility to set and uphold boundaries for their children, as well as enforce discipline when rules are bridged. They are rarely loved for doing so. Understandingly, some parents are abusive, and some children are victims of a parent's ignorance, frustrations, and bad fortune. Parents can also be bombarded with many concerns and personal issues that they sometimes lash out or shut out their children, which can affect children, leaving a lingering effect on them. Some actions or decisions parents make, or their lack can impact children negatively, such as divorce, child labor, overcompensation, under-compensation, too rich, very poor, too much attention (smothering), and lack of or little attention. Their effect on each child differs due to its severity and factors like culture, personality, and ability to adapt. But children should know that parents are humans and are not mistake-proof. At times, they act out of ignorance and frustration themselves. Children should also be aware that most of their parents' hardships are not self-inflicted. Their parents may have been victims of their circumstances or abused themselves. Also, what they perceived as abuse might be parents just making the best of their situation or repeating what they are familiar with. Truth be told, many parents today are victims of their children's abuse; they are verbally and physically, but mostly emotionally abused.

Many parents are being treated with disdain and taken advantage of by their children through their actions and non-actions. Therefore, many children can be said to be "toxic children" as they can be manipulative and controlling, unruly, defiant, and rude, resulting in many wounded, traumatized, heartbroken and confused parents. As no one situation is the same, I also struggle with assigning blames or some theories used for behaviors. I fail to understand the correlation between resentful or *bad* children on the one hand and poverty or bad parenting on the other, or equating good children to affluent or stable homes, as some had suggested. True! Instability, hardship, and bad upbringing can instigate bad behavior in children, but children from stable or wealthy homes, even those with a good upbringing, also go wrong. I have thought about stories where hardship has helped strengthen families or propelled a child's resolve to thrive and be better. In other instances, some abused children have also vowed not to be abusive parents themselves. Having said these, I believe that parents should also recognize their mistakes and apologize for them when a child's experiences hurt; they should also be made part of their child's healing process. An Igbo proverb states, "When you used one hand to discipline a child, you should use the other hand to soothe the child," suggesting that discipline and love should go simultaneously. I think this will be a good time to apologize to my children for the many times I acted out of ignorance or times I did not get it right.

To children, it is also imperative that they see their parents' point of view as well; they should also understand that a parent's reprimand most times comes from a place of love and not from a place of hurt. A parent's corrections might help them alleviate future mistakes that may lead to unpleasant consequences. "A stitch in time saves nine," or as an African proverb advised, "One should punish a child the first time he comes home with a stolen egg. Otherwise, the day he returns home with a stolen ox, it will be too late." Therefore, it is better to take heed now than face the music later. A parent's discipline is an act of love to help a child live a positive and fulfilling life in the future. Echoing Hebrews 12:5–7: "*My son, do not take lightly the discipline of the Lord and do not lose heart when He rebukes you. For the Lord disciplines the one He loves, and He chastises everyone He receives as a son.*" Endure suffering as *discipline; God is treating you as sons. "For what son is not disciplined by his father?"* Children should be mindful that in their resentment and anger that they don't dishonor their parents. The Lord recognizes that parents are flawed, yet he disapproves of dishonoring them.

Although today, parents who still try to enforce discipline are labeled as abusive, yet parents are mostly blamed for a child's misbehavior and problems. Some biblical scholars also accuse the parents of wayward children in the Bible as dysfunctional parents who provided no parental guidance to their children, thereby spoiling them and creating in them a feeling of entitlement. From the beginning, though living in paradise, Adam and Eve stumbled into sin for no good reason. God was a parent; he taught them good from evil, they didn't have external pressures or stresses, yet they fumbled. This is a lesson for us that ultimately, parents cannot be blamed for everything, especially for a choice their children made on their own. We cannot blame God for the sins of Adam and Eve, I think not.

There is no win for the parents; they are damned if they discipline their kids and damned if they do not. A writer responded to the one-sided approach of blaming parents for a child's problems by calling it a misnomer. Why do parents often take the blame for the bad and rarely get credit for any good? I wondered. I thought, though, dispiriting when one of my children will credit their friends with things going well in his life but quick to blame me for whatever was going wrong. Sometimes

I had to remind them sarcastically that as they did not just fall from the sky all grown, someone nurtured them up to the point of sudden independence, and those friends were nowhere to be seen then. Even when ill-advised from friends, siblings, and their act of free will backfires, it all comes back to parents. Igbos will liken it to a chicken who frowned at the cooking pot, but ignored the knife that killed it.

It is convenient for children to misdirect their aggression to their parents. What does one make of it when children themselves blame parents for their wrong choices or struggles, especially as adults? Considering that it is their reality, some attributed their struggles to the discipline they received as children. They claimed their childhood was stolen due to doing chores or helping with younger siblings. Some also attribute their difficulties or resentment of parents to restricting sleepovers or friendships as kids. Author Lidija Hilje pleads this case for parents:

> It seems a lot of people hold a lot of resentment towards their parents, blaming them for their limiting beliefs, lack of self-esteem, problems in their present relationships, and so on.
>
> A lot of people feel permanently marked by the scars that relationship with their parents left on their personalities. It really got me thinking. Should

we blame our parents for our insecurities as adults? What is the appropriate attitude towards the debilitating messages we have received from our parents in our process of growing up?

Is getting scarred by our parents—inevitable?

Human beings are born with a perfect sense of self... Babies don't have any problem with making their wishes known, which they do until their needs are met. There's no man, woman, politician, or religious figure who can convince a screaming baby to give up on their demands.

As we grow older, we learn all kinds of restrictions and limitations we have to adhere to. Our parents have the unfortunate role of pointing out all the imperfections of life—all the things we can't do, we have to do, we're not good at, we have to endure, and so on.

On the other hand, children have limited capability of critical thinking. As a result, they often fail to see the logic behind parents' words and actions, and jump to catastrophic conclusions. They generalize, and draw negative conclusions about themselves based on even casual comments or gestures…A child may interpret a simple gesture of re-making the bed after them, as: "you never do anything right," "you are incompetent," etc.

Umm! I thought about John Bevere's book *The Bait of Satan* on how satan uses offense as bait to trap people into grievance and unforgiveness. His analogies tie into a child's angry and resentful behavior toward parents. Offense to him is at the core of most disharmony and "the most difficult obstacle an individual must face and overcome." The scriptures also warn us that we cannot avoid offense (Luke 17:17, Matthew 24:10) but acknowledge, forgive, and heal from it. Offense is satan's most insidious trap to throw people off course and keep them in bondage by harboring bitterness against another. Offense, which manifests as anger, resentment, and unforgiveness, has led to psychiatric and psychological oppressions such as depression, anxiety, self-hate, isolation, disorientation, and vagabondism.

Eh! When grown children blame parents for their woes and difficulties, does it mean that they admit their wrong choices? What about personal accountability? I often wondered if the prodigal son ever blamed his father for his choice. Did Samson blame his parents for marrying an enemy against their warnings? Did he think his parents were racist, superstitious, or meddlers, perhaps when they were reasoning with him, did he blame them for not being more persistent? I also thought of Jabez, cursed from conception, yet no history of grudge was recorded. Instead, he took action that changed the course of his life. Abraham can be perceived as an abusive father; he disowned Ishmael and traumatized Isaac by almost killing him, yet no trauma or resentful behaviors were recorded. The circumstance of his birth was irrelevant when Solomon succeeded his father David as king, and he became the wisest man known. Moses's childhood should have created a lot of identity crisis issues for him, yet he rose to be a leader. We might say that these are just biblical stories; however, we have many stories like Oprah Winfrey's. Despite being a victim of molestation and a runaway who became pregnant at age fourteen, her predicaments did not deter or define her. Most are familiar with the quote "you are masters of your destiny" by Napoleon Hill.

Similarly, Steve Maraboli stated, "For most people, blaming others is a subconscious mechanism for avoiding accountability. In reality, the only thing in your way is you." These sayings then beg the question, so when is a child accountable for their actions? Not disregarding temperaments, the effects of adverse childhood experiences are real; however, people have risen above them to have good stability.

Reflections

Personal Growth: Blame Your Parents for Your Problems

> The differences between needs which ensure psychological and emotional survival and growth, and needs which arise from the neuroses, pathologies, and just plain whims of your parents and the environment and culture in which you are raised and have likely caused you considerable unhappiness and dysfunction in your life…you may blame yourself for not getting your needs sufficiently met as a child… You may have come to believe that you didn't deserve having your life-affirming needs met by your parents in a healthy way: These perceptions may have created in you a profound sense of inadequacy. Through your efforts to meet those needs in childhood and into adulthood, you have been attempting to prove your worth and demonstrate that you do, indeed, deserve to have your needs met.
> You didn't deserve to be treated the way you were treated and you don't

deserve it now. But it's not your parents who are treating you badly now, it's you. It is your life inertia—your thoughts, emotions, and actions aimed at fulfilling your needs—that continue to propel you down a bad path. So, being angry at your parents or trying to change them now isn't going to help you (you won't be able to change them anyway). You have to change yourself by taking responsibility for who you are now. You must make a commitment to let go of your needs and reconnect with your needs. Lastly, you must ensure that, though your life may not have been of your choosing as a child or on the path you have wanted up to this point in adulthood, you can alter your life inertia, so that is on the course you want for the rest of your life. (Jim Taylor, PhD)

Homeless to Harvard: The Liz Murray Story (movie)

The movie *Homeless to Harvard* was a true story of Liz Murray, one of two daughters of a terribly dysfunctional family in Bronx, New York. Her father is a loafer that whiles away his time watching *Jeopardy,* and he gets all the answers. Liz lived with her drug-addicted, schizophrenic mother, an intelligent father who was a drug addict, had AIDS, and her sister. She had to take showers in an overturned bucket to avoid using their bathtub that doesn't drain.

She was bounced from home to home as a ward of the state. At fifteen years old, she lived with her mom and her abusive grandfather, who sexually molested his daughters. Liz ran away with a school friend after an altercation with her grandfather. The turning point of her life was when her mother died, and her father moved to a homeless shelter. Her mother died of AIDS passed on to her from sharing needles. She was determined to finish high school, and she began attending the Humanities Preparatory School.

Despite all of her challenges and late high school start, she became a star student and finished high school in two years rather than the normal four years of high school. Through an essay competition, she earned a scholarship to Harvard. She later left Harvard to care for her ailing father but returned and now has a graduate degree.

Dr. Liz Murray, a wife and a mother of two children, is now a well-accomplished woman.

CHAPTER 9

It's a Conspiracy!

We desire to bequeath two things to our children: The first one is roots, the other is wings.

—African quote

The lies have been told that many parents try to force their children to succeed to make their parents look good. I am one of those parents that have been accused of such by none other than my children themselves. There are other accusations out there that parents also want their children to prosper for them. To that, I say, so what? I gladly accept. I wonder how that is bad and why I will wish my children otherwise. What is bad about reaping where you sowed? I don't want my children to be mediocre; also, I want them to succeed, excel, thrive, be successful, and be wealthy. I refuse to pay attention to the false narratives, which I consider inconsequential. Why will I wish them to be less? I ask that any parent who wishes or prays or encourages their children to be second-rated to please raise their hands. These are intrigues and fallacies of the devil, and they must be uncovered. They are part of his conspiracy to make us lose sight of what is important. I want my children to go further and do better than I did. I remember how I loved the name of my dad's age group, "Okanna," a proclamation meaning greater than their fathers (Okanna age group is a fraternity in my town for men born between 1931 and 1936).

In the Bible, the team King David sent to anoint Solomon as his successor proclaimed that his throne be even greater than his fathers', David. In their congratulatory message to King David, they prayed that God would make Solomon's name greater than his (1 Kings 1:37, 47). Every parent's prayer should be that their children do better than them. I had learned to dismiss the accusatory notions on my motives to help my children succeed; in fact, I totally embrace it. An Igbo proverb states that a child that washes his hands dines with kings, meaning that a successful or disciplined child will be counted among the nobles. I want my children to dine with kings. I will not apologize for wanting them to have the power to be in charge and not dependent on the mercies of others. Make no mistake, I am not one of those that pretend that money is not important. Although success is not all about money, however, success and monetary rewards most times go hand in hand. I also acknowledge that it also takes God's providence to be successful. Deuteronomy 8:18 declared that God is the one that gives us the ability to produce wealth, but I don't believe God rewards indolence. I believe that tenacity is faith in action for "faith without works is dead" and "a man is justified by works, not by faith only," according to James 2:14–17.

My thoughts drifted to a debate I had with my second son on why I often challenge them—meaning him and his siblings—to what they will refer mostly to as my "nagging." The conversation gave both of us an understanding that we lack prior and an opportunity for clarification. I understood that his problem was not with my "nagging" him to succeed but with his conceived perception of my interpretation of success. It is said, "To get oil from a nut, you have to squeeze it" (Igbo proverb). My message to my son (children) was, be your best, and don't limit yourself, for which he took as be someone else or have a particular career. I can't discount his preconception. Like his siblings, his truth was that I seldom show up for his soccer games (sports) and that of his siblings, while his friends' parents attend "all" their children's sports. He stated that I was more concerned about their academics and grades as I gave more time to those. He also saw my behavior as a common trend among most Nigerian parents.

Then he asked, what if sports made him happier, and what if he was better at sports than academics? I also mused about another conversation I had with his older brother, who expressed his difficulty in sharing with me that one of his best friends quit his high earning tech job to become a children's entertainer. While saying that, he was quick to add, "Mom, I know how you are. Before you start, he was very frustrated doing his tech job, but now he is very happy." The dialogue with my beloved sons was beside the point, and without prejudice to anyone's feelings or ideas, the truth is that I want my children to thrive and do well.

Success for me is also building a godly character and being in a position to effect change for the better. Though I had not gotten it right at times, my motives and drive are to raise dignified wholesome beings and for their struggles to be lesser than mine. The fact of the matter is that I aimed to help my children dream big, visualize themselves as winners, and know that they can live up to their full potential. I want them to fulfill their Jeremiah 29:11, a plan for a good future, and to fare well.

The book of Proverbs should be a comfort and a good tool for parenting. They provide antithetical parallelisms that defend the cause for instilling discipline, rightness, and integrity in our children. The nonsensical conceptions that attack parents raising their children to thrive and be their best are scams. The devil knows that another successful Christian is another threat to him and his kingdom. When Christians raise godly children, they position them to help make changes in society, and besides, it is a loss for the devil. My windshield in parenting is to ensure that my children revere God first, experience God's goodness on earth (Psalm 27:13), and live their best lives. It is difficult for one to live their best lives under subjugation; this is the reality of the human race and our world. Poverty, lack, mediocrity, self-doubt, defeat, accepting the norm, and the likes, are all subjugating tools of the enemy.

Though we are not of the world, we live in a world where poverty is an oppression; godliness alone will not put food on the table or pay bills. In the world I live, the people with authority dictate the rules and legislate the tenets we live by. As Proverbs 22:7 concurs, "The rich rule over the poor, and the borrower is slave to the lender." I often wonder why we quote scripture verses we don't believe for ourselves, or perhaps we are too pious to believe they can apply to us. Scriptures like Deuteronomy 28:13 states, "The Lord will make you the head and not the tail, and thou shall be above only, and thou shalt not be beneath." Another popular verse we profess is Deuteronomy 8:18, "Remember the Lord your God, for it is he who gives you the ability to produce wealth, and so confirms his covenant." I know God is concerned about my success and that of my children; it is in his covenant with us. I am also aware that the devil has perverted God's words and labels wealth and success as materialism. If God wishes us to prosper and gets the glory for it, then I embrace it unabashedly. Wealth is more in the wrong hands, and most of them are now role models for our children. I am amazed at how gullible and passive we tend to be at times. It is good to raise godly children, but better if they are armed to make positive changes and less dependent on handouts. I want my children to walk in authority, and I'm unapologetic in my desires for them.

As a parent, have you been accused of comparing your child to someone's child and vice versa? That, too, is a conspiracy of the devil. I thought of when I had been accused of such comparison even by my children. It is but half the truth and false perception that I rather not defend nor deny also. I have a strong feeling that I am being judged for this admission. Let me also note that I have not contradicted myself. I have earlier advised that the individualism of our children should be respected. Respecting children's individuality helps guide relationships with each child; it helps parents encourage their strengths, and in helping them maneuver through their weaknesses. Ephesians 5:1 charges us to be imitators of God in everything; it simply means to emulate what is right. Paul, in 1 Corinthians 11:1, asks the Corinthians to emulate him as he imitates Christ. Today, Paul may be accused of being pompous or blasphemous for that statement.

I look at things from a mindset of lessons to be learned and not comparing who is better. I look at stories of success and failure as lessons to motivate, challenge, or redirect. Success stories are supposed to challenge and are worthy of emulation, while that of failures should be a warning and a deterrent. As writer Edmond Mbiaka states, *"There is always something to learn from everyone you cross paths with because it's either you learn how to succeed or how to become a failure in life by looking at someone else's life."* We pray to God to show us signs, but sometimes the only signs we are ever going to get are observing the people we encounter or study. It is mostly about mindset and perceptions. A fixed mindset sees making references (not inferring) as putting down a child against another, or they aren't good enough. We ask our children to soar like an eagle and avoid pecking around with chickens. If you have said that, you are not making a comparison, but you are being judgmental, as these birds are a personification of people; therefore, emulate the eagles and hang with their likes and avoid the chickens. I grew up in an environment where parents ask their child with a less than an A (grade) if anybody in their class got an A. When the answer is yes, they challenge them to work harder next time to get an A, as it is proven to be doable. The motive is to let children know that the powers are in their hands, like the Little Engine that thought he could—to keep saying, "I think I can, I think I can."

The lesson there is optimism and hard work. It's all about mindset. Even before the Little Engine story, the Bible says in Romans 12:12, "be transformed by the renewing of your mind." Obama's presidency in a country like America for young blacks is not just to dream, but a realization that a dream nurtured can become a reality. Obama is what the church folks will call a testimony. I had wondered why I rarely hear the word *comparing* growing up. Kids in my days learn not only from instruction but mostly from observation. If someone gets into trouble doing something, you avoid that same thing, or the same trouble awaits you and vice versa.

As Christians, God has put what we need to succeed; all we need to do is tap into them. Have you ever thought to yourself why the Bible is full of stories? Why are testimonies encouraged, especially among us Pentecostals? What happened to Romans 10:17, "Faith cometh by hearing, and hearing by the word of God"? We need to start believing the Christian clichés we so often recite, and start applying them to our lives. Why do we have heroes and mentors? Why do we read autobiographies and memoirs? Why do we have history, fables, tales, folk stories, hymns, and folk songs? We increase our faith by hearing God's words: *Rhema* and *Logos*, the spoken and revealed word, and by testimonies—the *Dunamis*, the tangible demonstrated power of the word. The Bible also serves as a tool for equipping parents. In 2 Timothy 3:16, it is for teaching, rebuking, correcting, and a guide on righteous living. The devil will want us to believe that biblical stories are myths or that the gospel in the present age is void of power. When we do reference someone's story, is it seen as making comparisons? Yet, the Bible encourages us to share stories (both good and bad) for posterity, encouragement, or warning. Why do we learn stories in Sunday schools? The tales about David and Goliath. Why do we learn songs like "a wise man built his house upon the rock"? We reference stories of Jabez, Joseph, and Israel because they are stories of overcoming. Why do we teach about a little boy with five loaves and two fishes in John 6:9? Because it teaches us childlike faith and about surrendering the little we have as it is a vehicle for multiplication.

The comparison narrative propagated by society and some experts are conspiracies of the devil. An Igbo proverb warns that "the fall of a dead leaf is a warning to the green ones." The best safeguard is to learn from the mistakes of others, and a good road map will be learning from the successes of others. Remember the story of Eli and his children; was it ever a reference point to Samuel and his children? I had often wondered, or was it the case of the (stubborn) fly that did not heed to advice and followed a corpse into the ground (Igbo proverb)? Proverbs 14:12 states, "There is a way which seemed right unto a man, but the end thereof is the ways of death." One could only speculate, but because these biblical stories needed to be told, it might perhaps be a warning for us that God is no respecter of people.

Reflections

I remember asking my dad one day how people know that fire can burn and how people first know which plants are good for consumption and are not poisonous. His simple answer was that they must have seen someone get burnt by fire and witnessed someone die from eating a particular plant. In fact, he added, "I think it is by trial and error." I asked myself why I will opt for trial and error if I have a reference or if someone has set a precedence. In academics, especially in law and medicine, they cite precedence or research work of others most of the time. In fact, in academia, theories are studies agreed upon, challenged, debunked, and compared almost every day. Why can't we learn from the past?

Echoes

> History is filled with people who had been inspired to achieve great things through reading, hearing, or personal contacts with other great people. Everything in life is contagious, be it; success, failure, hope, or despair, can be contacted from a carrier. (Glory Emmanuel)

CHAPTER 10

A Critical Deception

> What to pass on. Legacy focuses on what will endure. It's about passing on things of lasting value to those who will live on after us. Legacy involves living intentionally and aiming to build into the next generations for their success.
>
> —Bill High

So! What if I had a motive?

I once heard it preached that every family should be a family on a mission heading somewhere, and they should be purpose-driven. The preacher affirmed, "Every family ought to be a mission; it has to be something." As a mission, it has to have a vision and/or a mission statement." My vision for my home is to build a Christ-centered, love-filled home. My mission is to raise respectful, accomplished, wholesome, and respectable individuals. To raise generation changers, kingdom builders—children that God will be pleased with, and I can be proud of. A mom that is less concerned about her children's well-being and a society that does not invest in their youth will be making a costly mistake and has been deceived. As I ponder on my role as a mother, I thought about biblical allegories that teach life lessons. In the parable of the sower, I saw parents as the sower and children as seeds that need to be sown on good ground (good upbringing) to produce good fruits. In the parable of the talents, I saw how God, the master, entrusts parents with children as an investment; they need to invest well to yield good dividends—children that honor him (Matthew 13:8, Matthew 25).

The more I thought about what legacy means to me, the greater my resolve to keep sharing my values and my desire to safeguard my family's legacy. In another sermon, I heard that God never expected us to be spectators in the affairs and stories of our lives. He also reveals his secrets—distinctions—to his children. Legacies are revelations of God, which are generational according to Deuteronomy 29:29, they "belong to us and our children forever," and therefore, they should have a generational impact. Being legacy-minded, therefore, is biblical. Deuteronomy 29 is God renewing his covenant with the next generation of Israelites that survived Egypt.

Heritage transcends the inheritance of wealth or a family heirloom. As Christian parents, what legacies are we building? What values are we passing down to our children? Legacies are strong foundations that go a long way to help build values and character, which in them takes work; they are created in pain, long-suffering, and sometimes in heartbreak. For posterity and continuity's sake, I purposefully ensured that I share my values to safeguard my pedigree (which has a generational impact) with the aim that the baton passes down to future generations. On his dying bed, King David charged Solomon to live right and keep God's commands so he can be guaranteed a successful life. He also asked his sons to be mindful of how they conduct themselves to ensure the continuity of their family's kingship legacy (1 Kings 2:1). I sometimes marvel when I ponder on some powerful stories I have heard. I have heard stories of the presumed "bad boys," men who, after so many challenges and wayward living, attribute their turnaround to values their parents or a parent figure instilled in them as children. They claim that these values never left them while in their bad ways but will convict them from time to time. "However far a stream flows, it never forgets its origin," says an African proverb. This adage is a comfort that when you know you have done your due diligence in raising your children, though they rebel, they eventually find their way back. Therefore, a legacy is much more than transient things, or things that may not withstand the test of time and can be forgotten.

I thought about the events recorded on 1 Samuel 13:19, the account of the Philistines, the age-old enemies of Israel, banning the craft of blacksmithing in Israel. It was recorded that no blacksmiths could be found in all the land of Israel. I wondered if the Israelites recognized this calculated yet dangerous tactic of the Philistines to end that legacy. The impact on Israel was grave as their source of defense was taken. The Philistines must have made the Israelites believe that the two nations were friends by lending them tools, which they still paid to borrow. They were not friends; they were frenemies, a notable character of satan the snake. Apart from the risk of being unarmed, blacksmithing in that era was a craft that was learned through apprenticeship and usually passed down family lines, thus affecting a family's business and their source of income. It is rightly said that our children are our future, meaning that they are our legacy. Affirmation of this idea is captured in some Igbo names like these: Nnamdi (my father is alive—seeing a son as a representation of his father) and Afamefuna (my name will not be lost or forgotten). In western societies, you have names like Trey and name suffixes such as Jr., III, and their likes, all suggest the continuity of the family. However, legacy transcends a name; it is something of value that we should take pride in and pass on. As is often said, "One is ever so eager to share what they take pride in and to safeguard what they deemed valuable," and the same goes for our values too.

Christian parents and schools are persecuted and hindered from creating and passing down their values. It is done openly by enacting new laws that are against our values, either in subtle ways through perversions or redefining them or by attaching negative labeling and stereotyping to our values. The redefinition of our values is one of the subtle ways the government aims to completely obliterate our Christian values; they make accommodations for everyone except Christians. Society and the new normal are now becoming the present-day Philistine. If our values and tradition are forbidden to be passed down to future generations, they will be lost. A lasting legacy must be enduring and embedded in the hearts of our future generations and heirs. God commanded parents to pass down family history and document them for reference. They should be set in stone as a memorial, and according to Joshua 4:6–7, *"When your children ask in time to come, saying, and 'what do these stones mean to you?' Then you shall answer them that the waters of the Jordan were cut off before the ark of the covenant of the Lord; when it crossed over the Jordan, the waters of the Jordan were cut off. And these stones shall be for a memorial to the children of Israel forever."* These records and history should also be part and parcel of a parent's manual and the fundamentals of a Christian legacy (1 Chronicles 16:12, Deuteronomy 6:7).

I relish moments when I have the opportunity to fellowship with my children and share our family history. One such moment was on Christmas morning of 2019. A conversation we had, took me down memory lane as I tried to share with one of my sons the stock he is made of and the great dynasty that is his heritage. As if by divine chance, I stumbled upon a recent online article, an interview by my dad, his grandfather. The interview covered over a decade of family history through a brief biography of him. My son's awestruck look and warmth at that moment assured me that he seems to understand some of my viewpoints, or should I add, he kind of understood where I'm always coming from. Like the Bible, in traditional Igbo society, our storytelling, dance, sayings, gestures, and even jokes are ways history was passed down and preserved, as well as the way morals were taught. The accumulation of these traditions is how we preserve our history that is also our legacy, which is the core foundation of our people, kinships, and nuclear families. Our tradition reflects the morals and social values that guide our people in their pursuit of a purpose-filled life and be good citizens. They are often performed in communal settings; thereby, they help foster collaboration, camaraderie, and shared values.

I also thought of my kindergarten days, the bedtime stories we read, the nursery rhymes we sang, and the poems we recited; most were metaphorical statements that also teach morals, respect, and kindness. Poems that discourage fighting and violence like this:

A Flashback

Isaac Watts

Let dogs delight to bark and bite,
For God hath made them so;
Let bears and lions growl and fight,
For 'tis their nature too.

But, children, you should never let
Such angry passions rise;
Your little hands were never made
To tear each other's eyes.

Although my children are now grown, I couldn't help but notice that most of what children read today are books on wizardry and magic. Their poems are now raps with adult languages that are not edifying. Most of what they watch today is violence; the era of *Sound of Music, Mary Poppins, Chitty Chitty Bang Bang,* and the likes seem to be over. Children are now disinterested in such musicals. They are bored with movies with no "real actions." Shows today are action-packed, meaning packed with violence, which are the usual way conflicts are resolved. How do you rationalize a five year old playing a video game that involves *shooting* a "bad guy" or thrusting them with a (weapon) sword? Is it also not surprising that our TV dramas and reality shows now are inundated with action for big ratings? They portray fights, flipping tables, throwing things, and shouting matches as ways to deal with disagreements.

God does not keep us in ignorance. When we invest in our children by training them, we are building a lasting legacy, and as Christians, a legacy that glorifies and promotes God but disappoints the devil. According to Proverbs 13:22, "A good man leaves an inheritance to his children's children, but the wealth of the sinner is stored up for the righteous." Wealth and material things are wonderful and much needed in the world's economy, but we should not lose sight of the mission. It comes in handy in promoting a kingdom agenda and helping to ease everyday life challenges. Material wealth is a wonderful thing to have, but it can be fleeting and not always dependable. It is powerless in protecting one from some unexpected life situations. If one can count on money alone, then wealthy people should never die from suicide, terminal diseases, or suffer from depression and anxiety. It is strange also that as bad as misfortunes are, they have become some family's legacy and are sometimes referred to as the curse or luck in these families. Bad lucks are not from God and do not glorify him. Sometimes, people keep themselves in poverty by thinking they are being humble or are serving God. Their false humility is a trap set by satan to keep them in bondage and misery; they have been deceived. We need to unmask the devil by taking back what is rightfully ours, our prosperity, but more especially our homes, starting with our children. We should recognize that the values we sow into our children now will ultimately affect their lives and many more generations to come.

Children are gifts that keep on giving; they are investments to nurture with an expectation of dividends. Just like a promised dividend on investments, they are good returns on investment, our secured and lasting legacies.

Legacy Mindset: Faithfulness

> Faithfulness is the heart of legacy. It is the idea that we'll be faithful with what we've been given. God has entrusted financial resources, but He has also entrusted us with far more valuable things: our families and our ability to influence them (and others) for good.
>
> When faithfulness becomes our core, our possessions become secondary to a higher priority: thriving children and families. God has called us to be faithful to pass on our values to our children and grandchildren. (Bill

High, CEO of the Signatory: A Global Christian Foundation)

Reflections

Today, if we don't intentionally pass a legacy consistent with our beliefs to our children, our culture will pass along its own, often leading to a negative end. It is important to remember that passing on a spiritual, emotional, and social legacy is a process, not an event. As parents, we are responsible for the process. God is responsible for the product. We cannot do God's job, and He won't do ours. (Focus on the Family, January 1, 1996)

CHAPTER 11

An Arrow in a Warrior's Hand

> Like arrows in the hand of a warrior,
> So are the children of one's youth.
> Happy is the man who has
> his quiver full of them;
> They shall not be ashamed,
> But shall speak with their
> enemies in the gate.
>
> —Psalm 127:3–5 (NIV)

Bows and arrows are common weapons used in ancient times for security (combat, protection, and defense) and hunting for food (sustenance and preservation). They are mostly offensive weapons used by trained warriors to fight opposition and ward off invaders or intruders. Psalm 127:4 tells us that as parents, we are warriors and our children, our missiles (arrows, battle-axes, and instruments) of defense, offense, and preservation. A warrior, according to the dictionary, is a fighter, a soldier, a combatant. In the olden days, a warrior is said to be an experienced or a seasoned fighter. The comparison of parents to warriors suggests that we are in a battle, and it is on account of our children. We need to be their fortress, and as children are compared to arrows, we also need to ensure that they are good ammunition.

I thought about arrows and what gives each their character, and how they are formed to become weapons. An arrow is just a stick that has been purposefully fashioned and carefully shaped, ready for flight when launched. They are fashioned to be battle-ready and are not ornaments to be showcased or hold on to as we mothers sometimes do. But the essence of parenting is to get our children prepared to face the world when they leave our homes at the right time. Fashioning an arrow for flight takes time and patience to make it effective and ready to be launched. It takes a whole lot of long-suffering, and it requires cutting and shaping. Forming an arrow to be efficient as a weapon requires a lot of calculation, resilience, and molding, just like parenting. As a mom, my responsibility is to shape my children, knowing that the process requires cutting, sometimes sanding, shaping, and even reshaping at times, although it is a painful experience. Also, all sticks are not the same, and some are bent or crooked; this is true of children. As a bent stick requires more attention to be formed, for some children, more attention, time, tact, patience, and re-fashioning are needed. These may be necessary, and ultimately more pain inflicted. As parents, we are required to train our children in the way they should go and not spare the rod (Proverbs 22:6, Proverbs 22:15, Proverbs 13:24), but in doing so, we should also be mindful of their uniqueness. We need to cut where and when it is required, straighten when needed, knowing fully well that the process can sometimes be challenging, unpleasant, and tedious.

Children will also try to resist, sabotage, and rebel during the process and will resent their parents; however, the process is necessary. But, as suggested by this Igbo proverb, "One cannot refuse to go to war because killing is involved." In other words, the consequence of not engaging tends to be more costly. A warrior's arrows must be sharp, straight, foster height and distance, and able to penetrate. It is unlikely for an unfashioned stick to hit or hurt its target. Arrows have to pierce their target to attain the expected result, they must be sharp—have substance, and they must be straight—character. Our children have to be equipped with training and should be positioned to be productive and also lead. They need to be able to soar like eagles and live above the smog of this world. They must be balanced and forthright to withstand opposition and capable of hitting and penetrating their target without missing (Matthew 10:16, Psalm 97:10, Ephesians 6:10, Proverbs 23:5).

But, children often will want to dictate how they want to be parented or the type of arrow they want to be; most times, they think they know better than their parents. As the clay cannot tell its maker how to make it (Isaiah 45:9, Romans 9:21, Isaiah 29:16), parents should not be taking parenting lessons from their children. Children need to be trained and guided while under our care. As parents, we need to begin this while they are young and impressionable, and easily adaptable. An African proverb advises, "A stick is straightened while still young." This principle is supported in Proverbs 19:18: "Discipline your children while they are young enough to learn. If you don't, you're helping them destroy themselves." Children need to understand their temporary discomfort is to help make them be better human beings. Romans 8:18 agrees that our "present sufferings are not worth comparing with the glory that will be revealed in us."

Psalm 127:5 calls a man with many children happy because they provide for him a sense of confidence while facing confrontation. In some traditional cultures, a man with many children is said to have loads of ammunition as he does not stand alone. A common saying among the Igbos is that "a man with many brethren is greater than the man with much wealth" or the name "Maduka," affirming people or families as an arsenal of weapons.

What then is a warrior without an arsenal? In 1 Samuel 13:19, there were no blacksmiths in Israel.

They had no tools or weapons, but they had able-bodied men. The scarcity of weaponry in an entire country meant they were powerless and open to assault. The Israelites relied on their enemy, the Philistines, to borrow or sharpen their tools at a non-negotiable price, as they now have the monopoly. Talk about inequality and vulnerability! Israel's fate now lies in the hands of the Philistine. They depend on them for their means of sustenance, as they need tools for farming, hunting, and security. The imagery of an entire nation bare of weapons is like the story of the Pied Piper, who lured all the children of Hamelin out of town, except three physically challenged ones. Imagine the Israelites as Christians and their children, weapons, while the Philistines represent the non-Christian faith. This portrayal shows the importance of children in our lives and the importance of having one of our own (also through adoption). Figuratively, Igbos will often say that one of the worst things that can happen to a man is having no one to mourn him or bury him when he dies. Culturally also, children are supposed to take care of their aged parents later in life, which used to be the normal circle of life. A similar scenario was stated in Ecclesiastes 4:8: "Consider someone who is alone, having neither son nor brother. There is no end to all of his work, and he is never satisfied with wealth. 'So for whom do I work,' he asks, 'and deprive myself of pleasure?' This, too, is pointless and a terrible tragedy."

I heard a sermon that gave me another perspective on children as arrows. The preacher shared how other religions believe in having lots of children as their tool for evangelism. He cited the following statistics from the 2018 Wiki to support his argument: *"Muslims have the highest fertility rate of 2.9 children on average per woman and above their replacement level, followed by Hindu at 2.4 children, Judaism at 2.3 children per woman and the others (including Christians,) have fertility levels too low to sustain their populations and would require converts to grow or maintain their size."* In some traditional cultures, arrows were shot with burning material attached to them, causing a fire to ignite wherever they hit. This exemplifies the spreading of revival fire when we launch our children like arrows to the world (Psalm 120:4, Isaiah 49:2). Therefore, it becomes much more than an individual thing. Our children can go further than us. Collectively as the church, they will accomplish more than we ever could; it is people that are the church, not brick and mortar—Maduka. People are worth more than possessions. I thought about the history of the Igbos. Traditionally, Igbos were mainly subsistence farmers, and they relied on their family size for labor. More children equate to a bigger workforce. A man's wealth was measured not only by the size of his barn but in the number of his children, as the two go hand in hand. A mighty warrior typically will have a large family, and his family is a microcosm of great villages and towns. The family or town or kin with the most able-bodied men were revered and feared by their neighbors as they stood in an advantage to defeat them in times of war or dispute, agreeing with our scripture verse. Such a man is fortified as his children provide for him camaraderie, solidarity, and confidence, and a majority advantage over an aggressor. These notions provoke Igbo names like Igwebuike (majority is power, strength in numbers) and Adigwe (short for "adigwe-emelie-dike"—with the majority you can defeat a strong man or, strength in numbers) or Obodo dike (the town of warriors).

Although the Bible also agrees that there is strength in numbers (1 John 4:4, 2 Kings 6:16, Leviticus 26:8, Deuteronomy 32:30, Matthew 18:19–20, Ecclesiastes 4:9–10), however, large numbers will be of no use without a united front. According to the Mongolian emperor Genghis Khan, "Not even a mighty warrior can break a frail arrow when it is multiplied and supported by its fellows. As long as your brothers support one another and assist one another, your enemies can never gain the victory over you. But if you fall away from each other, your enemy can break you like frail arrows, one at a time." The Bible also talks about the power of agreement in Ecclesiastes 4:12: "Though one may be overpowered, two can resist.

Moreover, a cord of three strands is not quickly broken," while other scripture verses warn about the danger of disunity (Matthew 12:25, Mark 3:25, Amos 3:3). Therefore, it is not surprising that the greatest tactic of satan is to bring disunity through discord, offense, and unforgiveness. All nations and creeds start with the family structure; satan longs to disintegrate the family unit by creating disorder and disunity, making our children easy prey for him. satan wants us to be at odds with each other, and he wants our children to be rebellious and vagabonds to destroy their destinies. One of the most disheartening experiences for a mother is dealing with a struggling child. As John 1:4 states, "I have no greater joy than this, to hear my children walking in the truth." God delights in obedient children and takes dishonoring parents very seriously. Those who love the Lord are wise and bring honor to their parents. The command to obey one's parents permeates scripture, and the only commandment with a warning is honoring parents (Exodus 20:12, Deuteronomy 5:16, Ephesians 6:2). Therefore, parents as skilled warriors understand that their arrows have to be in top form in other to thrive—fly and be progressive—hit their target with precision when launched. Echoed in 2 Samuel 22:15, "He sent out arrows, and scattered them." An arrow with character and precision represents a respectful child who is a great joy to his parents. Children are valuable as arrows; they are our heritage, God's tool for advancing our future; they are proposed to crush the head of satan. As such, to have children is to have a future; God also calls them seeds because they are God's promise for the future, seeds that will keep multiplying throughout generations to come.

LABOR PAIN

Echoes

A Letter from Jim Elliot to His Parents
(He died as a martyr on the beaches of Ecuador.)

> Grieve not, then, if your sons seem to desert you, but rejoice, rather, seeing the will of God done gladly.
>
> Remember how the Psalmist described children? He said that they were as a heritage from the Lord and that every man should be happy who had his quiver full of them. And what is a quiver full of arrows? And what are arrows for but to shoot?
>
> So, with the strong arms of prayer, draw the bowstring back and let the arrows fly—all of them, straight at the Enemy's hosts.
>
> Give of thy sons to bear the message glorious, Give of thy wealth to speed them on their way, Pour out thy soul for them in prayer victorious, And all thou spendest Jesus will repay.

CHAPTER 12

Labor Pain: Personal Growth

I know God will not give me anything I can't handle. I just wish that he didn't trust me so much.

—Mother Teresa

Labor pain is said to be tops on the list of pain for women. "Normally, the human body can only endure 45 units of pain. Yet at some points in labor and childbirth, a mother can withstand 57 units of pain, which is similar to 20 bones being fractured at one time," according to an article on babycenter.com. The pain of childbirth has also been compared to the pain a parent experiences over the heartbreak of a delinquent or troubled child. However, travailing through the pain and discomfort of labor gives birth to things of significance and value. This laborious effort, among other things, requires long-suffering and, most of all, wisdom. Wisdom—its definition often includes the application of knowledge and experience. While knowledge is simply learning, training, or understanding, experience, on the other hand, is a personal encounter, reality, and participation. Therefore, wisdom for me equates to growth, long-suffering, and fortitude. Motherhood was and still is one of my biggest teachers of wisdom, which often stem from painful experiences. It is often said, "No pain, no gain," and I agree as wisdom is usually a by-product of pain. Wisdom itself births growth, which embodies all our experiences, increases knowledge and opens up resilience, understanding, or empathy.

Genesis 22 was the account of Abraham's attempt to sacrifice Isaac, his son. Though we did not know his inner thoughts and feelings on his way to sacrifice Isaac, it must have felt like an emotional roller coaster. It was spiritual childbirth for Abraham; he experienced labor pain (heartbreak) with each step (contraction) he took to the labor ward (the altar of sacrifice). His reality at the time was that he was on his way to push out a stillbirth. That preconceived idea must have made his heartache worse. The closer he gets, the more intense the contraction and pain.

Nonetheless, he endured the journey by obeying God, and God did not disappoint him. The lesson here is that we have to trust God's words and his promises over our children, even when the journey seems painful and our perception, gloomy and hopeless. Proverbs 11:21 is an assurance that "the seed of the righteous shall be delivered." Abraham trusted God; he travailed and pushed forth his second delivery of faith, for which he was richly rewarded. That experience must have given Abraham increased insight into God's character as a promise keeper and Jireh. It was another growth opportunity for him as he increased both spiritually and materially. In raising children, there will come a time when they will have to leave our homes, irrespective of the timing, even as wayward and prodigals, as parents, no matter how painful or hurt we may feel at the time, we need to trust God.

Parenting is also like pregnancy; the embryo depends entirely on its mother for everything, and it has no say so. As the fetus develops and grows, the need to assert its autonomy. That process creates frictions and agitations for both mother and baby; the restlessness ultimately triggers contractions. Contraction then induces painful labor by which the baby gains its freedom from his mother's womb. Therefore, parenting can be likened to the womb experience; as children grow, the need for their independence intensifies. This usually creates conflict and discomfort for them and their parents. Just like contractions, these discomforts do intensify with each stage of growth and may present themselves as rebellion.

Although it is not easy, I have learned that it is sometimes okay to let nature take its course by trusting God and surrendering the situation. Trying to control the unpleasant situation of rebellion may feel like a wild goose chase. Parents have to stop the physical pushing (engaging) when the baby is already out. We must know that we can no longer raise grown children. Rather, it will be a good time to switch tactics and push in prayer. We are told to train a child; at adolescence and upward, parental guidance becomes limited and, most times, unwelcomed. Trying to parent, especially a young adult, most times, is calling for trouble.

Moreover, at that stage, a parent should have already preached, said, corrected, and done all they know how to do, and the children themselves must have also heard it all. Most parents go through different periods of spiritual contractions in various stages of their children's lives; sometimes, our faith is put under trial as parents. Travailing through it often leads to wonderful life lessons and a hope of a positive outcome or reward. Those lessons might be for us as parents, for our growth or for others, for ministry, and importantly, for the child—for their maturity. It is usually challenging for a parent and very disheartening when a child strays, but some children will only learn life lessons that way. This understanding now helps me pick and choose my battles with my children. To learn and grow through the easy and difficult experiences. I also realized that I cannot play the messiah nor do the work of the Holy Spirit. It's best to learn from the father of the prodigal who just watched and prayed, and Abraham, who trusted God and His promise.

Common sense is also knowing when to reassess or find a better means within one's control to tackle relationships and disagreements or hold one's peace. Growth also comes from accountability, personal assessment, and a change of mindset. It is doing things differently when necessary. Thus, I realized that most of the contentions and conflicts with my children stem from our cultural differences and pulls. Cultural misunderstanding is at the core of most dissension between families like mine. In my home, it is, in some cases, my perceived defiance and disrespect from them and their perceived idea of me as obdurate and too conscionable. This struggle is not just from raising our children in one's culture outside of our cultural environment, but also from understanding cultural differences and finding ways to maneuver some of them. And, doing so without losing our values or being at perpetual odds and provocation with our children. Cultural struggles are high in emigrate families raising children in an environment with different sets of values from their native cultures or family principles and moral beliefs. Cultural clashes have created serious issues in most homes like mine and have alienated children from their parents. Cultural issues are not simply a choice between good and bad, but that of relativism. Cultural relativism begs the question, "Of whose relativism?" And today, what is right or wrong has different interpretations, depending on who you ask, thus debatable. Similarly, both parents and children often struggle and deal with the stresses of acculturation, as motives are usually misunderstood on both sides. To most parents, there is a struggle with ethnocentrism that comes from the fear of their children losing their values, or them, the parents, dropping the ball as it pertains to passing down their legacy. For children, some researchers have claimed their struggles are from the confusion and the stress of balancing multiple cultures. Children are said to be torn and conflicted at times and may feel inadequate trying to balance two cultures. Cultural pulls can hurt children; the built-up tension when unacknowledged, mislabeled, or when a parent remains determined can trigger rebellion, resentment, and often emotional, as well as physiological conflicts in a child. However, from my experience, these narratives are more prevalent in western cultures. In the environment I was raised, although children are not necessarily exposed to opposing cultures, religious tenets of honoring parents also support the Igbo culture of respect and obeisance for elders.

As moms, we have to remind ourselves, especially when we are powerless, to change our children's behavior, to stop pushing. Moms may just have to travail in prayer, surrendering to God. Trusting the process entails having faith in their nurturing and hopeful in the expected end promised by God. As Jesus exemplified by ignoring culture when he healed on a Sabbath; parents need to fight (mostly spiritually) for their children rather than nurse their hurt or contend with culture or legacy. While prayer is important, however, wisdom needs to speak to us (Proverbs 8:1–9). Wisdom speaks, instructs, and teaches; it calls for understanding in navigating cultural differences. I thought of the advice I got from an older African colleague who opened my eyes to all the stresses children go through in the United States, unlike my situation as a kid in Africa.

Contrary to how I grew up, children in the US are pulled in so many different directions. There are sports, homework, lessons, recitals, school, and work. It does not end there. Then comes the community service, college applications, college essays, AP exams, SAT, ACT, scholarship applications and essays, school visits, them deciding on college majors and courses, worrying about tuition, going to school and working at the same time, and the rat race continues. Those are endless routines and competitive struggles to get ahead even as children—I feel dizzy now thinking of all these. These hustles were right in front of me; I was no stranger to them, but I didn't even notice their effect until they were pointed out to me, as stress triggers in children. As an immigrant parent, I have to understand that my children grew up in an environment different from the one I did and that our childhood orientations are also different. I did not have all those stresses growing up. All I owed myself and my parents were good grades. It was just school and home. School fees and work were adults' problems. For most like me, their first work application or experience and paying bills were after college. I now understand and appreciate my children's struggles better, and I've become more empathetic. It also opened me up to engage them in open and honest dialogues for our mutual understanding when the opportunity arises.

"What one does not know, to him, is like the night [darkness]" (Igbo proverb). As Christians, we tend to attribute every unpleasant situation as bad or of the devil. That will be accrediting the devil with too much powers. Besides, most things we don't understand or agree with may not necessarily be bad. In the past, I had felt trepidation over my daughter's strong disposition. I still have some concerns; however, a general conversation with a friend gave me another perspective from my preconceived apprehensions. I now see how her strength in character has emboldened her and how it can help her reach her highest potential and navigate our cutthroat world if used appropriately. It is not to accept or tolerate defiance as "teens will be teens" or a tool for disrespect or rebellion, but I now ask God to use that audacity for good works. That, too, was another eye-opener. So, through the discomfort, I have to learn to breathe (surrender) and push (in prayer).

My children had helped grow my resolve. Philippians 4:13 used to be another familiar Bible verse to me until motherhood. I had no idea how resilient I could be. My children are primarily why I had no option other than to keep putting one foot in front of the other, getting up each day, and venturing out even when I don't feel like it. Just like a woman in labor, who doesn't give up, and with each intensity of the contraction, musters enough energy to deepen her breathing and pushing. A full realization came while dealing with an old friend that went through a very challenging situation. He got knocked down and gave up on life. Like him, I survived a painful ordeal as well, although not a similar experience, but I could have easily got stuck in my misery. The difference between my friend and me was that he had no kids or dependents. His situation helped me recognize that it was not my faith alone that helped me through the trauma, but the fact that I am a parent and that my children are dependent on me for their entire well-being. Therefore, I did not buckle under the weight of it all. I had no choice. My kids were young at the time, and I was a single parent, which didn't leave me with much of an option.

Parenting is a very selfless calling. The true test of self-denial comes when you have to forgo mostly anything for the benefit of others. My children supersede my own needs and wants, and they had to be the bigger part of almost all my considerations. Selflessness became second nature to me—the lack of rest, sleep, personal cares, dinners, lunches, the protein shakes, the change of clothes in the car, the little naps, and assignments completed in-between runs, yet, a new strength kept on coming every morning. Philippians 2:3–4 states,

LABOR PAIN

"To do nothing out of selfish ambition or vain conceit, rather in humility value others above yourselves, not looking to your interests but to the interests of others." Parenting did that. I had to put my children above my wants and needs. Parenting, I believe, happens organically as I had no prior reference, and it is not typically a learned vocation.

Parenting taught me bravery—how to face my fear and not run from them. My children had, on occasions, forced me out of my comfort zone and helped me to be more assertive in my demands. My daring middle child taught me true courage in the face of danger and how to stand in one's truth. He is a constant reminder not to buy into my fears; nothing seems to faze him, and I still wonder how he can just be that nonchalant. A Roman philosopher Marcus Cicero states that "courage is the virtue which champions the cause of rights." I am convinced that Chichi, my middle son, will not budge from his truth even in the face of a terrible outcome. He also will not let injustice deter him from his goals. I witnessed him unfazed, going through a scheme against him. Instead, I was the one losing sleep over the incident. Amidst the ordeal, he kept on winning. Embarrassingly, I was the one who buckled under the strain of his ordeal. To date, anytime I bring up the situation, he has to remind me that he doesn't remember it until I bring it up. That particular situation also helped me gain more confidence in my children and trust how I raised them and God's word concerning them.

One of the most significant growths in my life I attribute to motherhood was overcoming the spirit of judgmentalism. This was a big growth moment for me. Before the unfortunate surprises from my children, I had a very critical spirit and a condemning attitude. I had to repent from those because they were equally hypocritical. My Google search result defines judgmentalism as "thinking of ourselves morally superior because we haven't committed the acts of others." Another definition was "assuming things about someone without looking at the situation from every point of view." No wonder the Bible instructs to remove the log in one's eyes before removing the speck in others. As we Igbos say, "When the pallbearers are carrying another man's dead child, an unrelated onlooker thinks they are carrying coconuts."

Sometimes, we cannot feel or relate to other people's situations until we experience them ourselves. Like labor pain, which is hard to explain to someone who had not gone through it, one must experience it to understand it. Not only did I repent, but I now have more empathy, tolerance, and understanding toward people, even if we act and behave differently. I now understand why it's difficult to judge anyone when you have not walked in their shoes. Now and then, when the critical and judgmental spirit creeps up, I quickly take authority over it and repent from it. I also learned that I could disapprove of behavior but never a person. Also, as a mother of two boys, I now understand the plight of young black men in America. Having grown up in Nigeria, I could not understand or truthfully appreciate their daily challenges until my sons became victims of racism. Being children of African descent with African names, they were also victims of xenophobia from teachers, which started early from elementary school. One of my regrets was that I did not recognize it sooner, as I did not know what it was. I also did not believe my children then or supported them effectively the way a guardian should. This is one of my regrets as a parent; however, it made me realize that parents can be ignorant at times and not above error.

As I had made mistakes as a parent, I had to extend grace to my parents. This does not mean that I agree with all my experiences growing up, but I realized that parents are humans and not God or superheroes. As a child, I did not know that parents struggle at times and that they have challenges. Because it never affected me, I had no cause for concern. Life seemed fine. Hakuna Matata. There are no troubles. It is customary for parents to provide for their children; that is the order of things. I didn't realize life comes with highs and lows because lack or insecurity never crossed my mind. In my culture, we say that "A child traveling on his mother's back doesn't know how far the journey is." As a child, I didn't know that parents go to bed every night and wake up every morning burdened, knowing that they have to hustle to provide as lives depend on them. This is notwithstanding what was going on in their lives. Parenting has taught me that parents don't always have it right all the time, and it should not always be our way or the highway. Parents do make mistakes; whether by ignorance, negligence, or carelessness, our best intentions might end up not being good ones.

I also learned how to be persistent, especially in my demands, a trait my daughter helped cultivate in me, a relatable lesson to the parable of the unjust judge (Luke 18:1–8). When I vehemently argued against teaching my daughter to drive as that experience did not turn out well, especially with her oldest brother, she wouldn't listen. My spirited daughter, who witnessed my experience with her brother, was not having it, even when I suggested paying someone to teach her. This child refused to buy into my excuses and remained adamant. She would always say, "You are my mother. You are not asking anyone, and you will teach me how to drive." She badgered me into submission and got me out of my comfort zone, and indeed, I taught her to drive without meeting our demise. Naturally, I am not a thrill-seeker, and I try to stay away from anything that will cause me unnecessary anxiety, like teaching people to drive. After overcoming the driving lessons, this child then demanded that I take her for her driving test too—that to me was asking just too much. I pleaded again that my presence could make her nervous as she will feed into my fear. Not her, no! She goes. By some miracle, she won that too. Now, I use her tactic and mimic her boldness when praying, and I sometimes quote her in my prayers by telling God that he will have to come through for me as he is my father. I became more persistent and bolder in my prayers, according to Hebrews 4:16.

As a mother, the fruits of the spirit (love, joy, peace, patience, kindness, goodness, faithfulness, gentleness, and self-control) had become a daily exercise. They had become labor pains I had to push through regularly. Long-suffering or patience is not one of my strong suits, but motherhood has made me succumb. If I did not have children, it might still be a huge challenge for me to practice patience. As a determined mom to strong-willed and driven children, it could get exasperating sometimes. My only option was to enroll in the academy of Christian virtues, which I also call "baptism by fire." I am a little above average in patience now, but that is far from where I started. People often say, "Let go and let God"; I often pondered on this saying. And, they don't add that it is easier said than done. They also fail to educate on its practical application. How does one let go if it pertains to their children, not things or other relationships? When is the right time to let go? What does letting go really look like? Does it mean stand and watch your child sink in despair or self-destruct without interfering? I still worry, and I am still concerned and sometimes angry and frustrated.

I have also heard that worrying equates to faithlessness. When a mother's heart is hurting for a troubled or an estranged child, even though she prays about the situation, does it mean she has no faith? The father of the prodigal son was anxious and did not hide his feelings; he was troubled, he got up daily, hoping for his son's return. When the mother of Moses knew her son was in imminent danger, she took action and did not wait for fate. In Genesis 37:35, Jacob was determined to continue grieving for Joseph until death. Hmm! What can we deduce from the actions of these parents?

Surrendering

By experience, I know that God has the ultimate and the final control. He shows up unimaginably for my children and me. Even with our biblical stories, I don't think it was the parents' worrying that led to the outcome in these stories. It could be their trust in God, which propelled their actions that forced God to move. God knows the end from the beginning and his outcome, which is for good.

Through the challenges of motherhood, the contractions, and the labor pains, I learned the lesson that even if it was never said, "Let go and let God," my powers are very limited. I had to learn to forget what is behind; letting go of past errors, the pressure, the old wounds; and forgetting the undesirable and not making them my forever reality but learning from the place of my failures. As Philippians 3:13–14 states, "Brethren, I count not myself to have apprehended: but this one thing I do, forgetting those things which are behind, and reaching forth unto those things which are before, I press toward the mark for the prize of the high calling of God in Christ Jesus."

In pain, there are gains. Yes! In good times, children teach philia (affectionate love); they bring cheer, joy, respect, and honor. They give us the zeal to survive and the will to persevere at tough times. At all times, they teach us agape love, and they help us grow. Children are a reward. They inoculate our lives with significance, and they help us grow closer to God. Parenting itself is an institute of continual learning.

The Pencil and Eraser Story

Once upon a time, the pencil and the eraser were having a conversation about each other's jobs. Both of them were praising each other for their hard work, but they knew that they needed each other. Soon the pencil began to draw a straight line and soon lost its balance and ruined the straight line he was creating. The pencil got very mad because he knew the eraser would have to suffer for him to correct his error.

The pencil said to the eraser, "I am sorry," but the eraser, who did not know what he was talking about, asked, "For what?" The pencil replied, "I am sorry that you get hurt because of me. Whenever I make a mistake, you are always there to erase it. But as you make my mistakes vanish away, you lose a part of you, and you get smaller each time." On hearing this, the eraser replied, "That is true, but I don't really mind. You see, I was made to do this. I was made to help you every time you did something wrong, even though one day I know I will be gone. I am actually happy with my job. So please stop worrying! I will not be happy if I see you sad."

There are five things you need to know. Always remember them and never forget, and you will become the best pencil you can be.

- *You will be able to do many great things, but only if you allow yourself to be held in someone's hand. (Allow yourself to be held in God's hands and allow other human beings to access you for the many gifts you possess).*
- *You will experience a painful sharpening from time to time, but you will need it to become a better pencil. (By going through various problems in life, you become better.)*
- *You will be able to correct any mistakes you might make.*
- *The most important part of you will always be what's inside.*
- *On every surface you are used on, you must leave your mark. No matter what the condition, you*

must continue to write. (Leave your mark wherever you go, no matter the situation, and continue to do your duties.)

The pencil understood and promised to remember and went into its box with purposes in its heart.

Thoughts on the Story

Parents are like the eraser, whereas their children are the pencil. They're always there for their children, cleaning up their mistakes. Sometimes along the way, they get hurt and become smaller and older and eventually pass on. Though their children will eventually find someone new (spouse), parents are still happy with what they do for their children and will always hate seeing their precious ones worrying or sad.

All my life, I've been a pencil. And it pains me to see the eraser that is my parents getting smaller and smaller each day. For I know that one day, all that I'm left with will be eraser shavings and memories of what I used to have.

A children's story.

CHAPTER 13

The Travail: Spiritual Growth

> I'm proud of the woman I am today because I went through one hell of a time becoming her.
>
> —inspirational motivational quotes

Parenting is travailing; it's painful and laborious, like giving birth. It's the contraction, the labor pain, the breathing, the push, which perseveres to birth a predestined outcome—a metaphorical analogy best described in Galatians 4:19. And it states, "My dear children, I am suffering the pains of giving birth to you all over again—and this will go on until the Messiah takes shape in you."

The mother-child dyad reflects our relationship with God as well. The Bible attests to that fact, with many comparisons of God's love for us, his children, to that of a mother's love (Isaiah 66:13). It also speaks about the "Nacham" or the disappointment God feels when we, his children, sin (Genesis 6:7–9).

Motherhood has made God's feelings about me more relatable both in my proud moments and when I disappoint him. His love, agape love, becomes more understandable to me in a new way. Like I want my children to be wholesome, so does God, and that is why Jesus paid the ultimate price for mankind—loving us without condition, no strings attached, and enduring. Despite my willfulness, rebellion, bad attitude, or disenchantment at times, I see how God has not stopped loving me as I will not stop loving my children no matter their shortcomings. I also see how I can be ungrateful and unappreciative of God at times, not because I lacked manners, but because I have gotten too familiar with his love. Like mothers sometimes feel unappreciated and taken for granted, God feels that way when we show him disdain, ingratitude, silence, and our feeling of entitlement. True to the saying "familiarity breeds contempt," I know how disrespectful it can be. I now appreciate God more, especially when I have been impossible, unlovable, accusatory, and rebellious. God feels, and he hurts the same way children's rebellion hurts parents. Motherhood made that fact relatable.

Like children sometimes want to dictate the tone of the relationship with their parents, I had done the same with God. Similarly, I had their same reasons:

he does not understand, his ways are either too hard or dated, he is just too old, and he's from a different era. Like children, I prefer God's pampering, comforts, and provisions to his discipline and my reluctant obedience. Most times, my acknowledgment of Him as a good parent is being blessed, and I expect him to be a "yes man" to my demands. As soon as I don't have my way, I whine, sulk, and get salty. As a mother, I can relate to the times I expect God to be at my beck and call (frankly, I still do), but I get defensive and offended when he requires my attention. Motherhood also convicted me of being a prodigal at times, as I had often rebelled or wanted things my way. Truthfully, like children, at times, I blame God for my bad decisions, which I do with excuses or justifications to support my claims. I had actually blamed God for not trying hard enough to stop me from a mistake I made that the warning signs were very palpable. Do those sound familiar? Experiencing similar attitudes from my children led to soul-searching moments when I recognize that sometimes I act out like a child toward God.

Also, it feels good when our children show they love us. I have not only loved my children unconditionally, but I have also received love from them. I know we love each other even though, at times, we are at odds with one another. The most powerful weapon my daughter uses to disarm me or gets the best of me is her display of unconditional affection. The Bible says to give thanks in all things. I learned that the best time to "Hallel and

Barach" God is in tough times and times I'm not asking him for something. Like a child, we expect God to meet our every need and grant our every wish like a fairy tale Genie. We demand it and exactly how we want it. However, we forget that he knows what is best for us like any good parent does. This realization convicted me of sometimes overindulging God, yet I often take his provisions for granted. The reasoning is that as a parent, he is obligated to cater to my needs. That was my thinking then. In an epiphanic moment, I gave myself a sarcastic pat on the back, remembering when I got the same sentiment from my children. The times I thought, "Surely they must feel very entitled," with no concept of appreciation. I learned a lesson on thankfulness—to be intentional in appreciating the *little mercies*. Interestingly, I also see my manipulative moves and attempts to guilt God into buying into my demands. As a mom, I do not have to look far to see reflections of my witty smarts and emotional blackmail looking right back at me. God knows, and he understands as parents do. "Before Abraham, Jesus was," as the saying goes. Although God sometimes chooses to remain silent, he is the ancient of days, and we cannot outwit him. It's the same with parents. Also, as a parent, I realize that God doesn't owe me anything, even though occasionally I may think he does. Well! In a moment of one of my deep thoughts, I caught myself asking, "What have you done for God lately?" A question children should sometimes ask themselves about their parents, especially grown ones.

In the same way, parents hurt over a rebellious or prodigal child, God also hurts over his wayward or backsliding children. Like a parent to an older child, he will not impose his will on us or force intimacy with us, but he patiently waits for us to repent and return to him. This, too, is a lesson in long-suffering and patience. One of my sons recently discovered the Serenity Prayer and posted it in our group chat. I think the prayer sounds good; however, some of the words, in my opinion, are not biblical as it takes God out of its context. Accepting things that seem insurmountable to man according to the verse of the prayer counters 1 Peter 5:7 that states to "cast all your cares on him (God) because he cares for you." God can make what seems impossible with man possible, according to Luke 18:27.

Since we are talking about labor pain, let's look at Jabez. His mother had a record-breaking labor pain that she literally cursed her child. Jabez's fate seems to be sealed; it seemed he was doomed to a life of struggle and misery, and he can rightly blame his mother for it. He did not pray the Serenity Prayer or resolve to his fate; he solicited the one who can change his situation—the "I Am." He travailed in prayer, and God prospered him, and now we have the "Prayer of Jabez." His prayer has changed more lives than the so-called Serenity Prayer. It has taught us not to accept the status quo. Also, if the mother of Jabez, through a name, impacted her son's life negatively, in that case, it is then a testament that a mother's prayer can effect a positive change in her child's life.

Some people resolve to find peace in their challenges or learn to accept them, but does a mother really find peace with a troubled child or a troubled relationship with a child? I thought about the saying, "It's not over until it is over," and the word *hope,* and what they both connote—does hope denote wishful thinking? While still thinking of a way to respond to the group chat without provoking negative sentiments, I thought of King Hezekiah, whose death seemed a foregone conclusion (Isaiah 38:1–5 and 2 Kings 20:1–6). Should one ever give up hope or stop trying? If so, King Hezekiah's Serenity Prayer should have been this: *"Lord! Into thy hands, I commend my spirit."* "What gave him the impetus not to accept that fate?" I asked myself. Perhaps he was familiar with Ecclesiastes 9:4, "While there's life, there is hope"—Ndubisi (living or life is paramount). Still alive, he took that opportunity and acted. The prayer of quitting sounds reasonable and soothing, it may not be for the audacious, and I find it void of God's word and power as well.

Zechariah 4:9 alone deflates that thinking, it affirms that challenges can be surmountable, but not by our might or power, but by the spirit of God; we have a higher authority. Understandably, overcoming takes travailing. Travailing is endurance, and it's not for the faint in spirit; however, the good news is that God is in charge (of our lives and destinies). Thus, Isaiah 38:1–5 affirmed that we could level any mighty mountain (challenges) before us. Notably, my favorite verse is God's declaration to Zerubbabel; He said that because his hands laid the foundation of the temple – meaning Zerubbabel's hands, therefore, will also complete it. I claim the same as a mother. As parents, we started the foundations of our children's lives, and we must have a say-so in completing who they become, not friends, peers, culture, or society.

Likewise, Matthew 19:26 concurs that man has his limitations: "But with God, all things are possible." The same way I have faith that nothing can separate me or snatch me from the love of God, I have faith in the promises of God concerning my children. Besides, that same promise is for them too.

My Sincerity Prayer

God, grant me the Sincerity
to cast my cares on you, who can cause
the change I need;
Courage to trust
in your promise of a good outcome; and
Wisdom to know my peace
comes from you.

Parents are at a loss as to why a promising child suddenly starts acting out of character. They should not be alarmed or easily dismiss the strange behaviors as stereotypical of children or a result of puberty. There may be more to the behaviors than meets the eyes. Solomon laments in Ecclesiastes 10:7 how he saw slaves on horseback, while princes go on foot like slaves. That right there is anomalous. Unrecognizable behaviors most times are red flags; satan is a coward and often masquerades himself. He and his earthly minions mask their attacks as psychological, mental, and behavioral problems; they are often behind vagrancy, self-denigration, aloofness, anger, dejection, depression, and their likes. With this knowledge, as parents, we ought to stop contending with our children but use that energy to take authority over the spirit behind strange behaviors.

Parenting is warfare. As a mother, I have learned to be more spiritually aware. Again, raising children initiated me automatically in the academy of spiritual warfare. The saying "a foe can take you farther than an ally" is a truism. Being a mother has helped improve my prayer life; it has turned me into an intercessor and made me more prayerful. There is no love lost between satan and me; therefore, I had to be proactive and offensive in my prayers than just wait to dodge his attacks. The fight over our children's destiny is not to be fought carnally, and prayer is our weapon to destroy every evil plan over them (Ephesians 6:12 and 2 Corinthians 12:4). Parents have the authority to stand in proxy for their children and refuse to let satan run amok in their homes by bringing disharmony or mess with their children's future. If unchecked, our foe's delight is to steal, kill, and destroy (John 10:10–29). He will not only use our children to cause us pain but achieve his ultimate goal of destroying their destinies.

Matthew 11:12 advises that the violent take it by force, so I refuse to be complacent. Jesus exemplified the importance of intercession; thus, he is seated at the right hand of God, our father, actively and perpetually interceding for us. As his imitators, we ought to do likewise for our children. Despite his finished work on the cross, Jesus did not take a sabbatical; he is still working on our behalf, and likewise, a mother's work is never done. As an Igbo proverb states, "Eneke-nti-oba [a bird] says that since men have learned to shoot without missing, he has learned to fly without perching." Therefore, since satan is busy and relentless in his pursuit, mothers should also be travailing in prayer. They should continuously be on guard. If the devil could come after Jesus, then our children and families are no exception. As written in James 5:16, "The effectual fervent prayer of a righteous man availeth much." We should pray in and out of season and "in the spirit on all occasions with all kinds of prayers and requests," according to Ephesians 6:18. Therefore, I pray for my children's God-given destiny, their education, godly mentors and spouses, against ungodly friends and associations, their protection, a sound mind according to 2 Timothy 1:7, and importantly, their salvation.

Parenting also helped develop my prophetic and priestly gift. I learned to speak into my children's life, calling out their God-ordained destiny. As the head and the authority over my children, I continually speak into their lives in the good times and times of disagreement, anointing them and making declarations, calling forth their Jeremiah 29:11. I also learned not to dismiss any thoughts or hunches concerning my children but to pray when I have those feelings. As a mom, I recognize that these are a few of the ways God sends us signals.

My children have also helped me become a better witness and evangelist. Philemon 1:6 commands that we share our faith as it becomes "effective for the full knowledge of every good thing that is in us for the sake of Christ." Who better to share the good news with than our children? Deuteronomy 6:6–9 commands that we testify to our children always and as often as possible. My life generally is and has always been a testimony that my children are part of. I make sure I share my testimonies; they are the first people I witness to. A pastor friend of mine asked my first son, who was about eleven at the time, to write a letter that she will read to children on her mission trip to Haiti. My son encouraged those children, telling them that Jesus will change their situation. He then concluded by telling them not to believe their current situation because the "devil is a liar." At the time, that phrase "the devil is a liar" was my go-to expression, and I did not know that he picked up on it. In 1 Corinthians 11:1, Paul told the Corinthians to follow his example as he follows the examples of Christ.

Equally, the Igbos say, "When a she-goat chews her cud, her kids watch her mouth." Our children watch us and will try to mimic our actions. While in sixth grade, my second son demanded that I close out his little savings account at the bank as he would like to tithe all his savings; likewise, his sister gave away a new Bible I just bought for her to someone she thought needed it more. I remember that at the time, I was teaching them about tithing and seed sowing. I would also make one of them put our offering inside the giving envelope, and another will drop the envelope into the giving basket. God, honoring his words, a week after my son gave away his little savings, he got a check in the mail, a forgotten investment. He stood in front of the entire church on children's day that year to give his testimony. Knowing children listen and observe us gave me more confidence and enthusiasm to be a better witness of the gospel.

I am also amazed at how children unequivocally trust their parents practically for their existence. As I watch my children rely on me for all their daily provisions in an insentient way, I questioned why I couldn't trust God the same way. Lord! How can an adult live out Matthew 6:31–32, which states, "Therefore don't be anxious, saying, 'What will we eat?' 'What will we drink?' or, 'With what will we be clothed? For the Gentiles seek after all these things; for your heavenly Father knows that you need all these things." Is it even possible?

I'm often mesmerized by how children go about their day unconcerned about their needs, trusting that they will always be met. They don't worry or fret over whether they will have food, shelter, or clothing, knowing their mom has to provide and that she will. I don't think the word *need* exists in their little world. If it is not believing in their parents to take care of their needs, then I don't know what faith looks like. Why do children lose their trust as they grow? Maybe grown-ups analyze things a lot as I do, I thought. Is that why we don't have childlike faith? Perhaps, unlike children, adults can be too critical of themselves and may think they are unworthy to receive from God. Umm! I thought about my children. No matter how naughty or bad they have been or how angry I am at them; that doesn't stop them from helping themselves with what they want from the fridge or in the house. On both the good and the not so good days, they will still eat, have a bed to lie on and clothes to wear, as well as other bonuses, like being chauffeured, their activities paid for, school supplies provided, and the list goes on.

I often wondered what Jesus meant when he said, "Suffer little children to come unto me, and forbid them not: for of such is the kingdom of God" (Matthew 19:14 and Luke 18:16). I wondered if there was a correlation between a Christian's suffering for their faith (pain, resentment, disillusion, disagreement, rejection, condemnation, etc.) to the travail of a parent. Also, why does the kingdom of God belong to people like children? With these in mind, motherhood played a role in building my faith and increased my dependence on God, understanding and appreciating more the enduring nature of God's grace. I also learned from children to be less self-condemning and try to stop overanalyzing how a need will be met. An awareness that to trust God more meant a deeper relationship with him.

The gift of children helped me strive to leave a Christ-centered heritage or legacy. One centered on honor, diligence, service, benevolence, compassion, and one that reverences God. The scripture is against those that will not build into their family; it refers to them as unscrupulous and worse than an infidel (1 Timothy 5:8). Like in my culture, legacy is important to God. The Bible speaks about goodly inheritance, family, and name. Those matters a lot, and people strive to maintain good names for themselves and their families. Who is your daddy or family? That question becomes very important. "A good name is to be chosen rather than great riches," proclaims Proverbs 22:1 and Ecclesiastes 7:1. Pedigree matters and godly parenting helps with cultivating a disciplined life and a thriving heritage.

Although it is often uncomfortable and painful at times, no one likes to be disciplined, and a parent also does not take pleasure in disciplining. However, like a parent, the Lord disciplines those he loves (Hebrews 12:6) for the "the rod of correction will drive away foolishness" (Proverbs 22:15). I learned from being a mother that God corrects us out of love. He chastises us like any responsible parent would, as a preventive measure, to save us from or stop future problems. Have you ever heard the phrase "it could be worse"? His chastening at times is his way of correcting and covering our errors and also a way to redirect us. It may be painful at the time, but in hindsight, we see it was ultimately for our good.

Echo

> The Bible tells us repeatedly in his word how all children are a gift from God. Every single life, every single child, is a reward and blessing. Whether they're bringing parents pride and joy or whether they are teaching us how to be more patient and forgiving, children are a gift from God and a source for the growth of his kingdom here on earth.
> God knows that children can bring us closer to Him and help grow our Christian character. (Bible Study Tools Staff)

Humor
What Did God Do after Adam and Eve Sinned?

A while back, I asked my daughter about the Garden of Eden. She's only 10, but she's heard that story many times. And I wanted to see what she'd understood from the story. She got the "sin" and "consequences" part just fine. But when I pressed a bit further, things didn't exactly go as expected.

Me: What did God do after Adam and Eve sinned in the Garden?

Daughter: He punished them.

Me: Yes, but what else did he do?

Daughter (after a long pause): Um, he tortured them?

Okay, that wasn't exactly what I was looking for (and I also need to find out what she's been reading lately). But I can understand her problem. Apparently, we'd done a great job talking about God's disappointment and righteous anger in the garden. But we'd completely neglected making sure she understood how much more there was to the story. And I think many of us do the same. We see the wrath, but we miss the grace.

LABOR PAIN

What did God do when Adam and Eve sinned? I think he showed grace from beginning to end. (Marc Cortez)

MY FINAL THOUGHTS

> A successful parent is one who has loved, one who has sacrificed, and one who has cared for, taught, and ministered to the needs of a child. If you have done all of these and your child is still wayward or troublesome or worldly, it could well be that you are, nevertheless, a successful parent.
>
> —Howard W. Hunter

I thought I had matured, but I could not claim that status until I became a mother. I thought the devil had hit his best shot, but no! Not until I had children. I thought I was a warrior—oh no! Until motherhood made me a guardian.

Frankly, I have weighed situations from every angle I thought of. I asked lots of questions on what I could have done better, or what I did do wrong, as well as what I didn't do or shouldn't have done. I had sometimes wondered if things could have been different for my children, specifically if their dad was present. I thought about what the outcome would have been if they grew up in Nigeria. *What will that different look like?* I wondered. What if the difference left me with questions too or wanting more?

Well! Well! I have to confess that I did not have it worse. This book is also a gift I am giving myself. God does not make mistakes; he didn't give me more than I could bear. Truth be told, I was favored. As I begin to hear myself through my writing and my meditations, my thoughts turn into appreciation and positive affirmations. I heard myself saying, "God forbid that I would murmur like the Israelites who wanted to go back to Egypt, according to the book of Numbers 40." It could be easy to lose sight of how far we have come and how he brought my children and me from a mighty long way. I paused apologetically and let out a calming sigh. And he answered, "I did not intend to bring you thus far to leave you. That, my child, is not in my character. Keep holding my hands." It was then a sober reminder that God is on my side.

My thoughts and analyses though lengthy, they have helped me get to where I am now. Though some things may seem ancient and irrelevant today, there is an underlying denominator in my discoveries relevant both then and now. It is in Matthew 11:12, which states, "From the days of John the Baptist until now, the kingdom of heaven suffers violence, and violent men take it by force." Since God cursed satan in the garden of Eden and said that the seed of a woman would be against him, it was game on. We need to know who the real enemy is. 1 Peter 5:8 revealed satan as an adversary. However, most see him no more than a medieval boogeyman, as I used to, and we treat him as such. I know that satan is so scared of the human seed that he works overtime to destroy or corrupt them; he declares all-out war on children, sometimes from the womb. I never truly cared much about spiritual warfare and thought that people who engage in them were either paranoid or just extra; as a mother, that ignorance ceased. It is said that "hell has no fury like a woman scorned," and I add, mess with her child, hell is unleashed with one mad warrior mother. Proverbs 8:36 warns that those who wrong me wrong their own soul, and those who hate me love death. Though it seems harsh nonetheless, it is scriptural. I don't know about you, but my children are off-limits. That is where I draw the line.

May I speak to the readers? You need biblical clarity, and you need to believe every word in the Bible. Why do I say these? God laments that his own perish due to ignorance (Hosea 4:6). Knowledge is power. In this context, it helps us know who our enemy is and teaches us how to arm ourselves. According to 2 Corinthians 2:11, awareness helps "so that we are not outwitted by satan," and in my culture, we say, "It is not cowardice to be on an alert." When you can say that you raised your kids to the best of your abilities, then you have a right to question strange behaviors. Simply put, "If it looks like a duck, swims like a duck, and quacks like a duck, then it probably is a duck."

Because satan is no boogeyman, let us then examine scripture. Scripture reveals satan's vocation; he is a thief, a killer, and a destroyer, and he roams around seeking who to waste (John 10:10, 1 Peter 5:8). Don't take my word for it; just read the book of Job. There was no provocation whatsoever from Job, yet, he was afflicted; satan was just doing his job. We know his attributes. satan is not timid and no respecter of persons; he cost Saul and Samson their greatness and their lives, he tempted Jesus, and dared him a second time by infiltrating his disciples Peter and Judas. He is not flesh and blood; he is a principality and high-level wickedness.

The mad man of Gerasenes is a testament—see Mark 5:1–10. And satan is not omnipresent but guess what? He uses human agents and demons, the likes of Judas, Delilah, Harman, Ahitophel, and Potiphar's wife. As fairytale stepmothers portray, one of his most effective tools for initiating his human agents is envy. Does it surprise you that the Bible unmasked envy as witchcraft? Please know that someone not familiar with you cannot be envious of you, and as satan is not omnipresent, it makes sense that your enemies are very close, mostly household wickedness. We know that we are not fighting people but the spirit behind their behaviors; therefore, we need to redirect our anger and aggression from our children to the real enemies. The Bible tells us that "the heart of man is deceitful above all things, and desperately wicked" (Jeremiah 17:9). People are wicked, and not everyone wants us or our children to thrive. As earlier stated, there is no need for provocation. For example, Envy is not a person but a spirit, and it gives birth to legions of other wicked spirits. Our enemies are too close; it penetrates our homes, relationships, and our environment.

We need to examine the environment we raise our children in, and what or who they are exposed to, like traditions, popular culture, social acceptance, and even religion. Some influences are territorial demons in operation like those that functioned in Sodom and Gomorrah and eventually led to its destruction (Genesis 18:20). These same demons are present in our nation today. There are territorial curses, too, like the plague in Egypt in the book of Exodus caused by their abuse of the Israelites. In the United States, we had the Curse of Tippecanoe or the twenty-year presidential curse, an alleged pattern of deaths in the presidency in which occurrence was evenly divisible by twenty; it was said to result from the crimes against Native Americans.

It is common knowledge that every curse has a cause, which is sin. Sin gives satan the legal right for a curse to thrive; curses often create strongholds. They are recurring and create generational problems. After exploring our environment, we need to look inward, on bloodline issues. There are family curses, familiar spirits, or ancestral spirits (ancestral spirits can also be territorial). They result from the sins of the fathers. Scripture declares, "The parents have eaten sour grapes, and the children's teeth are set on edge" (Ezekiel 18: 2 and Jeremiah 31:29). Humans are still paying for the sins of Adam and Eve, the first parents of mankind. The world is still paying for the sin of Abraham through his two descendants Isaac and Ishmael.

Let's look at an example of a relatable bloodline issue and generational curse in one family, that of King David's. He lacked self-control and succumbed to lust; he coveted what belonged to another man, his wife, just because he can. As sin begets sin, he turned into a liar, a schemer, and a murderer. These are the consequences of one mistake that started with lust and ended up polluting an entire bloodline through several generations. Also, polygamy made the setting perfect for the saga that followed. Ammon, David's son, raped his half-sister due to lust and lack of self-control and died for it (2 Samuel 13:1–39). Absalom, another son, died contending with his father due to his scheming and covetous spirit (2 Samuel 15:1–6, 18:1-18). Adonijah followed in the same footsteps of his brother Absalom and coveted the position of his half-brother, Solomon. He, too, died for it (1 Kings 2:12–25). Solomon, in all his wisdom, thought it was okay to marry unbelievers. Lust, evil entanglement, lack of self-control, and polygamy was at work. It got worse; his women initiated him into idolatry, another name for occultism (1 Kings

11:1–13). In the third generation, David's kingdom began to disintegrate. His lineage was only able to hold on to one kingdom, Judah (Benjamin later merged with Judah), out of twelve kingdoms through Solomon's son Rehoboam. Ten of their kingdoms went to Jeroboam, their former employee, who Solomon attempted to murder (1 Kings 12:1–19). Later, their only kingdom, Judah, was captured and exiled in Babylon. Scripture made it clear that God visits the iniquity of the fathers upon the children up to the third and fourth generation (Exodus 20:5). Today, these curses manifest as hereditary problems as with family medical histories like diabetes, mental and emotional problems like anxiety, rage, and behavioral or relational difficulties like alcoholism. A well-known bloodline issue in America is the Camelot curse. Each time tragedy strikes, Americans do ask, "Why does tragedy stalk the Kennedys?"

Thank God that curses can be broken. For a nation, the answer is in 2 Chronicles 7:14: "If my people, which are called by my name, shall humble themselves, pray and seek my face and turn from their wicked ways, then I will hear from heaven, and will heal their land." For us, once identified and exposed, it can be broken through Jesus Christ. Therefore, we need to trace our children's problems through their bloodline and deal with them from their roots. Like Gideon, he was a child of destiny but did not know it. The angel that came to him nearly gave him a heart attack by addressing him as a "mighty man of valor." At the time, nothing was great about him; he was a wimp and from a wimpy bloodline. He had to tear down his father's altar of Baal, and he also raised a personal altar to Jehovah God to come into his ordained destiny. He not only redeemed himself but his family and his cursed nation from the Midianites (Judges 6). Children at times suffer for things older than them that originated from their parents and forefathers. I declare that my children will not suffer from the sins they know nothing about or from inherited problems, in Jesus's name.

Our children are our future; they are predestined to help us win when we face our enemies and prevail on our behalf (Psalm 127:5). We are not to be afraid of the enemy. He was already doomed from the onset; he is a defeated foe. Knowing this will help us fight better. As parents, we have to be careful of the type of altars we are erecting and what we attract to our lives as they have generational consequences. We have to repent of our sins and the sins of our fathers. We need to tear down any evil altars from all bloodlines and reject all evil curses from all our children's bloodlines. We have good news as Christians, we have a covenant with God, sealed in the blood of Jesus, and our victory is assured. We have to trust the Word of God wholly. Proverbs 11:21 tells us that "the seed of the righteous shall be delivered." I charge parents in the words of Nehemiah, "After I looked things over, I stood up [in the spirit] and said to [parents]…'Don't be afraid of them. Remember the Lord, who is great and awesome, and fight for your families, your sons and your daughters, your…[bloodline] and your homes'" (Nehemiah 4:14).

To mothers, stay focused, eyes on the prize. Your children's destiny is at stake. Arise and war, keep advancing in the thick of oppression. The stronger the challenges, the more glorious the win. "For if God be for us who can be against us" (Romans 8:31).

I, the Qoheleth, the assembler, the narrator of these thoughts, mark them as a memorial for all who have and who are yet to experience any form of labor pain (physically or spiritually). May it be a keepsake to all who have birthed, raised, or nurtured a child.

"May the grace of the Lord Jesus Christ, and the love of God, and the fellowship of the Holy Spirit be with you all" (2 Corinthians 13).

Reflection

> Children are blessing because they are one means by which God develops faithfulness within weary parents, they give parents "a sense of understanding and repentance."
>
> The birth of a child is "charged with transcendent meaning." Children are living affirmations that God's creation is good, and they compel us, like nothing else in life, "to serve a future

we cannot control" and to trust that God is not yet finished with this world.

They are free beings, independent agents who eventually will supersede us, living their own lives, not echoing ours. Having children thus involves a profound surrender, and children are often cause for anxiety. Parents want to educate their children and save up an inheritance, provisioning their progeny for the uncertainties of life. Of course, a wise person knows these efforts can come to naught: The Lord giveth and the Lord taketh away. Welcoming the gift of children requires trust in divine providence: "Let it be done unto me according to your word." (Luke 1:38, Evangelicals and Catholics Together)

Poem

On Children
Kahlil Gibran

And a woman who held a babe against her bosom said, Speak to us of Children.
And he said:
Your children are not your children.
They are the sons and daughters of Life's longing for itself.
They come through you but not from you,
And though they are with you yet, they belong not to you.
You may give them your love but not your thoughts,
For they have their own thoughts.
You may house their bodies but not their souls,
For their souls dwell in the house of tomorrow, which you cannot visit, not even in your dreams.
You may strive to be like them, but seek not to make them like you.
For life goes not backward nor tarries with yesterday.
You are the bows from which your children as living arrows are sent forth.

The archer sees the mark upon the path of the infinite, and He bends you with His might that His arrows may go swift and far.

Let your bending in the archer's hand be for gladness; for even as He loves the arrow that flies, so He loves also the bow that is stable.

187

When we trust in God's promises, we can counteract cynicism and doubt with optimism and belief.

—www.godtube.com

PRAYER FOR MY CHILDREN

Know therefore that the LORD your God is God; he is the faithful God, keeping his covenant of love to a thousand generations of those who love him and keep his commandments.

—Deuteronomy 7:9

Father, I come again to intercede for my children. I ask for forgiveness for my sins and the sins of my children. I ask that you cleanse my children and me with the blood of Jesus so that my prayer will not be an abomination to you and that satan will not have any right to accuse me. I publicly renounce the devil, and because I believe in Jesus, I am saved, and my children are saved according to Acts 16:31.

According to Isaiah 54:13–14, my children are taught by you, Lord, and great is their peace. They are established in righteousness, and oppression shall be far from them, as well as danger.

As the Lord declared, anyone that attacks my children will surrender to them. They shall surely gather, but whosoever shall gather together against my children shall fall for their sake, in Jesus's name.

The Lord who created the waster shall destroy any man or principality that seeks to waste my children's destinies. No weapon formed against my children will succeed according to Isaiah 54:16–17. I condemn every evil tongue that has risen against them.

According to Psalm 91:7–8, a thousand shall fall at my children's side, ten thousand at their right hand, but no evil will come near thee—my children, no harm or disaster shall befall thee nor come near thine tent.

Oh, Lord! Send out arrows, and scatter my children's enemies. Send forth lightning and unsettle them, according to 2 Samuel 22:15.

As the authority and a priest over my children, I decree and declare that any hoaxes, envy, evil eye, voodoo, sorceries, incantations, chants, and curses against my children shall boomerang, locate, and destroy their sender. According to Matthew 18:18, every evil arrow and evil load directed to my children, I return them to the sender, and I struck every monitoring spirit with blindness, in Jesus's name.

I come against any ancestral spirit, environmental spirit, and generational curses from my children's lineage. I break and destroy, in Jesus's name.

In Jesus's name, I break and destroy evil covenants and soul ties entered by or on behalf of my children through their bloodline or evil entanglements. I decree that they shall have no effect on my children. I sever these evil ties on my children. I bound and destroy them, by order of the fire of Elijah according to 2 Kings 1:10.

Woe to you, satan! The blood of Jesus is against you. Spirit of rebellion, offense, hurt, failure, stagnation, confusion, delay, the spirit of restlessness, anxiety, depression, mental oppression, ADD, ADHD, disturbance, deceit, fear, condemnation, and vagabondism, hands off my children. According to Acts 16:31, I command you to collide with the blood of Jesus and be destroyed.

Shame on you, satan! You are under my children's feet, according to Psalm 91. Be trampled, and my seed bruises the head of your demons, according to Genesis 3:15.

According to Ezekiel 6:3–4, I demolish and smash to pieces any high places, towers, and mountains standing in the way of my children. May the Lord destroy these high places, cut down their incense altars, may he pierce their owners with a sword, and heap their dead bodies on the remains of their idols, according to Leviticus 26:30.

I tear down every evil altar speaking against my children; I destroy every stronghold and strong man opposing them. By order of Gideon in Judges 6:28–29, I tear down every ancestral idol, deity, shrine, and occultism in my children's bloodline and ancestral home, in Jesus's name.

As the head of my household, I raise a superior altar for my family by replicating the altar of Noah in Genesis 8:20, and I declare this: May the Lord smile on it and bring fruitfulness and prosperity to my children, may my children move forward, in Jesus's name.

According to 2 Samuel 24:18–25, I raise the second altar of protection over my children. May no pestilence, disease, or plague come near them or their dwelling, in Jesus's name.

According to Psalm 112:1–2, because I delight greatly in the Lord's commandments, my seed will be mighty upon the earth and blessed.

My children's lots are in pleasant places, and they have a good inheritance, according to Psalm 16:6. As a result, the wealth of the wicked is for them, according to Proverbs 13:22.

According to 2 Corinthians 5:21, my children are the righteousness of God in Christ, and because I believe in Jesus as Lord, therefore, my children and my household are saved, according to Acts 16:31. I obey the Lord; therefore, my children are blessed, and they will prosper abundantly.

Deuteronomy 28:3–14 says, my children are blessed in the city and in the county; they are blessed when they go out and come in. They have been set above nations, and they are generation changers, and I say amen.

The fruit of my womb will be blessed, their vocation is blessed, and whatever they lay their hand to do prospers, in Jesus's name, according to Matthew 18:18.

I thank God that angel goodness and mercy follow my children 24-7 according to Psalm 23:6, and angels are keeping charge over them, according to Psalm 91:11.

I cover my children with the blood of Jesus from the soles of their feet to the crown of their heads. I curse all symptoms of illness and any sickness and disease that tries to rise over them from their roots. Their body, mind, emotions shall function properly the way God designed them, in Jesus's name.

I thank God that they will fulfill their Jeremiah 29:11; therefore, I cover their stars with the blood of Jesus.

Oh, Lord! Continue to bless the latter part of my children's lives more than their former part. Bless their marriage and their children. May they see their children to the fourth generation and be full of years (Job 42:12–16).

My children will not die before their time as the Lord has promised to satisfy them with long life, according to Psalm 91:16.

My children are part of the church of God advancing, and no gates of hell shall stand against them. Because I declared, like Joshua in Joshua 24:15, that I will serve the Lord with my household, my children are saved.

Because I am in covenant according to Proverbs 22:6, my children will not depart from my teaching; they will bring joy to me and not shame, according to Proverbs 10:1.

As my love gift from God and heaven's generous reward according to Psalm 127, my children will arise to protect and nourish me in old age. They will have influence and honor to prevail on my behalf and victory when I face my enemies.

I cover this prayer with the blood of Jesus, and I ask God to commission an army of angels to see this warfare prayer through, in Jesus's name. And to deploy Archangel Michael to intercept every prince of Persia opposing these answered prayers from manifestation, in Jesus's name.

Lord, keep my children and their affairs in the circle of your wheel.

Thank you, Jesus. Amen.

THE MYSTERIOUS DILEMMA OF FIRSTBORNS

The Son is the image of the invisible God, the firstborn over all creation. For in him all things were created: things in heaven and on earth, visible and invisible, whether thrones or powers or rulers or authorities; all things have been created through him and for him. He is before all things, and in him, all things hold together. And he is the head of the body, the church; he is the beginning and the firstborn from among the dead, so that in everything he might have the supremacy.

—Colossians 1:15–18

Firstborns are important because they are the strength of their parents, and they validate them as fruitful. They are usually a parent's love child, and they affirm their masculinity or femininity. Jacob said this of Ruben, his firstborn: "You are my firstborn, my might, the first sign of my strength, excelling in honor, excelling in power" (Genesis 49:3). Firstborns represent two things: one is that they were born first, and the other is that they are marked for authority.

In the past, firstborns held significance in their families and communities. For the first male, they are the heir apparent, and they are the ones that will ultimately take over from their father and become the head of the family. In the Old Testament, firstborns receive the first share of inheritance and the blessing of a double portion (Deuteronomy 21:17). Also, a lot is expected from firstborns; the expectation is for them to do well as pacesetters or mascots for the family. The expectation is that if they do well, then the others following them will. They set examples and the tone for their siblings to follow.

Jesus is said to be the head of the body, the church; he is the beginning and the firstborn from among the dead, so that in everything, he might have the supremacy (Colossians 1:13–23). It is then not surprising that when satan could not kill Jesus as an infant, he tried to tempt him into relinquishing his authority. Therefore, it seems that controversies follow firstborns, from Ishmael to Abel to Esau and to Ruben and Manasseh;

their headship had always been in contention. Perhaps, the mixed up or the presumed preference of the younger over the elder in the Bible may otherwise be to confuse satan from killing their destinies.

Firstborns are significant; it took the death of the Egyptians' firstborn sons to get Pharaoh into submission by releasing Israel from slavery. God also did not spare his own firstborn to show the depth of his love for his other children, us. He gave up his most prized possession, Jesus.

PRAYER OVER FIRSTBORN

> Everything that opens the womb, of all flesh which they offer to the Lord, both of man and beast, shall be yours; however, the first-born of man you shall surely redeem.
>
> —Numbers 18:15

My firstborn son, the blood of Jesus, your sacrificial Lamb, has redeemed thee; therefore, you will not be anyone's sacrificial lamb.

You have been redeemed under a superior covenant, and the blood of Jesus always pled for grace over your life. As it is written in the Law of the Lord: "Every firstborn male that opens the womb shall be called holy to the Lord"; therefore, according to Luke 2:23, the Lord calls you holy.

I pray for you now as my firstborn child, my first son, and the firstborn in your father's house of your generation. I cover you with the blood of Jesus, and I declare, according to Exodus 12:21–23, that destiny wasters and destroyers will pass you by.

According to Exodus 12:19, may any oppressor, taskmaster, or pharaoh in your life that stubbornly refused to let you go meet the wrath of God at the midnight hour. May the mighty hand of Jehovah deliver you from any spiritual Egypt and any form of slavery, be it physical, mental, emotional, or financial, in Jesus's name.

Every aspect of your life is under the blood of Jesus; therefore, you are the head God ordained you to be, and you will never become a tail. You will never relinquish your position, as the first, or lose your birthright. You will never trade your birthright, and according to Proverbs 11:21, as my seed, you will go free, and according to Proverbs 12:7, you will stand firm.

My son, you will never borrow to eat, beg to sustain your life and that of your family. As the heir, you will live up to and fulfill your rightful duties as the firstborn, in Jesus's name.

As a redeemed and a covenant child of God, you are delivered from every satanic attack, household enemies, envy, and jealousy, in Jesus's name.

You will not sell, trade, transfer, or gamble with your position of preeminence, in Jesus's name. I take authority over the spirit of Cain, and I declare that your star will not be murdered, in Jesus's name. I take authority over the spirit of Jacob, Ruben, and Manasseh, and I declare that your firstborn blessing and anointing will not go to another, in Jesus's name.

You will pursue and overtake destiny robbers and recover every aspect of your birthright that was hijacked, in Jesus's name.

You will never bow or serve your juniors or subordinates in Jesus's name.

You will fulfill your purpose and God-given destiny. Amen.

Afterward, Samuel took a stone and set it up between Mizpah and Shen. He named it Ebenezer, saying, "Thus far the Lord has helped us."

—1 Samuel 7:12 BSB

BIBLICAL REFERENCES

And ye shall teach them your children, speaking of them when thou sittest in thine house, and when thou walkest by the way, when thou liest down, and when thou risest up. (Deuteronomy 11:19)

And thou shalt teach them diligently unto thy children, and shalt talk of them when thou sittest in thine house, and when thou walkest by the way, and when thou liest down, and when thou risest up. (Deuteronomy 6:7)

Train up a child in the way he should go: and when he is old, he will not depart from it. (Proverbs 22:6)

As it is written, There is none righteous, no, not one. (Romans 3:10)

Thus saith the Lord; A voice was heard in Ramah, lamentation, and bitter weeping; Rachel weeping for her children refused to be comforted for her children, because they were not. (Jeremiah 31:15)

Now the birth of Jesus Christ was on this wise: When as his mother Mary was espoused to Joseph, before they came together, she was found with child of the Holy Ghost. Then Joseph her husband, being a just man, and not willing to make her a public example, was minded to put her away privily. (Matthew 1:18–19)

And she brought forth her firstborn son, and wrapped him in swaddling clothes, and laid him in a manger; because there was no room for them in the inn. (Luke 2:7)

And when they were departed, behold, the angel of the Lord appeareth to Joseph in a dream, saying, Arise, and take the young child and his mother, and flee into Egypt, and be thou there until I bring thee word: for Herod will seek the young child to destroy him. When he arose, he took the young child and his mother by night, and departed into Egypt. (Matthew 2:13–14)

Then Herod, when he saw that he was mocked of the wise men, was exceeding wroth, and sent forth, and slew all the children that were in Bethlehem, and in all the coasts thereof, from two years old and under, according to the time which he had diligently inquired of the wise men. (Matthew 2:16)

And when they saw him, they were amazed: and his mother said unto him, Son, why hast thou thus dealt with us? behold, thy father and I have sought thee sorrowing. And he said unto them, How is it that ye sought me? wist ye not that I must be about my Father's business? (Luke 2:48–49)

And he was casting out a devil, and it was dumb. And it came to pass, when the devil was gone out, the dumb spake; and the people wondered. But some of them said, He casteth out devils through Beelzebub the chief of the devils. (Luke 11:41–15)

But Sarai was barren; she had no child. (Genesis 11:30)

And Isaac intreated the Lord for his wife, because she was barren: and the Lord was intreated of him, and Rebekah his wife conceived. (Genesis 25:21)

And when the Lord saw that Leah was hated, he opened her womb: but Rachel was barren. (Genesis 29:31)

And her adversary also provoked her sore, for to make her fret, because the Lord had shut up her womb. And as he did so year by year, when she went up to the house of the Lord, so she provoked her; therefore she wept, and did not eat. (1 Samuel 1:6–7)

And there was a certain man of Zorah, of the family of the Danites, whose name was Manoah; and his wife was barren, and bare not. And the angel of the Lord appeared unto the woman, and said unto her, Behold now, thou art barren, and bearest not: but thou shalt conceive, and bear a son. (Judges 13:2–3)

And her adversary also provoked her sore, for to make her fret, because the Lord had shut up her womb. And as he did so year by year, when she went up to the house of the Lord, so she provoked her; therefore she wept, and did not eat. (Luke 1:6–7)

Thou shalt be blessed above all people: there shall not be male or female barren among you, or among your cattle. (Deuteronomy 7:14)

And Sarah said, God hath made me to laugh, so that all that hear will laugh with me. And she said, Who would have said unto Abraham, that Sarah should have given children suck? for I have born him a son in his old age. (Genesis 21:6–7)

Now Elisabeth's full time came that she should be delivered; and she brought forth a son. And her neighbours and her cousins heard how the Lord had shewed great mercy upon her; and they rejoiced with her. (Luke 1:57–58)

LABOR PAIN

And they slew a bullock, and brought the child to Eli. And she said, Oh my lord, as thy soul liveth, my lord, I am the woman that stood by thee here, praying unto the Lord. For this child I prayed; and the Lord hath given me my petition which I asked of him. (1 Samuel 1:25–27)

And the angel of the Lord appeared unto the woman, and said unto her, Behold now, thou art barren, and bearest not: but thou shalt conceive, and bear a son. (Judges 13:3)

He delivereth the poor in his affliction, and openeth their ears in oppression. (Job 36:15)

And I will make of thee a great nation, and I will bless thee, and make thy name great; and thou shalt be a blessing. (Genesis 12:2)

And Noah awoke from his wine, and knew what his younger son had done unto him. And he said, Cursed be Canaan; a servant of servants shall he be unto his brethren. And he said, Blessed be the Lord God of Shem; and Canaan shall be his servant. God shall enlarge Japheth, and he shall dwell in the tents of Shem; and Canaan shall be his servant. (Genesis 9:24–27)

And Jabez was more honourable than his brethren: and his mother called his name Jabez, saying, Because I bare him with sorrow. (1 Chronicles 4:9)

And they journeyed from Bethel; and there was but a little way to come to Ephrath: and Rachel travailed, and she had hard labour. And it came to pass, when she was in hard labour, that the midwife said unto her, Fear not; thou shalt have this son also. And it came to pass, as her soul was in departing, (for she died) that she called his name Benoni: but his father called him Benjamin. (Genesis 35:16–18)

O Jerusalem, Jerusalem, thou that killest the prophets, and stonest them which are sent unto thee, how often would I have gathered thy children together, even as a hen gathereth her chickens under her wings, and ye would not! (Matthew 23:37)

Honour thy father and thy mother: that thy days may be long upon the land which the Lord thy God giveth thee. (Exodus 20:12)

Honour thy father and thy mother, as the Lord thy God hath commanded thee; that thy days may be prolonged, and that it may go well with thee, in the land which the Lord thy God giveth thee. (Deuteronomy 5:16)

Honour thy father and mother; which is the first commandment with promise; That it may be well with thee, and thou mayest live long on the earth. (Ephesians 6:2–3)

This know also, that in the last days perilous times shall come. For men shall be lovers of their own selves, covetous, boasters, proud, blasphemers, disobedient to parents, unthankful, unholy. (2 Timothy 3:1–2)

Thy wife shall be as a fruitful vine by the sides of thine house: thy children like olive plants round about thy table. (Psalm 128:3)

Be not deceived: evil communications corrupt good manners. (1 Corinthians 15:33)

And, ye fathers, provoke not your children to wrath: but bring them up in the nurture and admonition of the Lord. (Ephesians 6:4)

Fathers, provoke not your children to anger, lest they be discouraged. (Colossians 3:21)

He that spareth his rod hateth his son: but he that loveth him chasteneth him betimes. (Proverbs 13:24)

And Jacob said to Simeon and Levi, Ye have troubled me to make me to stink among the inhabitants of the land, among the Canaanites and the Perizzites: and I being few in number, they shall gather themselves together against me, and slay me; and I shall be destroyed, I and my house. And they said, Should he deal with our sister as with a harlot? (Genesis 34:30–31)

And it came to pass, when Samuel was old, that he made his sons judges over Israel. Now the name of his firstborn was Joel; and the name of his second, Abiah: they were judges in Beersheba. And his sons walked not in his ways, but turned aside after lucre, and took bribes, and perverted judgment. (1 Samuel 8:1–3)

And the firstborn said unto the younger, Our father is old, and there is not a man in the earth to come in unto us after the manner of all the earth: Come, let us make our father drink wine, and we will lie with him, that we may preserve seed of our father. (Genesis 19:31–32)

Now Absalom had commanded his servants, saying, Mark ye now when Amnon's heart is merry with wine, and when I say unto you, Smite Amnon; then kill him, fear not: have not I commanded you? Be courageous, and be valiant. (2 Samuel 13:28)

And there came a messenger to David, saying, The hearts of the men of Israel are after Absalom. And David said unto all his servants that were with him at

LABOR PAIN

Jerusalem, Arise, and let us flee; for we shall not else escape from Absalom: make speed to depart, lest he overtake us suddenly, and bring evil upon us, and smite the city with the edge of the sword. (2 Samuel 15:13–15)

And when he had removed him, he raised up unto them David to be their king; to whom also he gave their testimony, and said, I have found David the son of Jesse, a man after mine own heart, which shall fulfil all my will. (Acts 13:22)

And it was so, when the days of their feasting were gone about, that Job sent and sanctified them, and rose up early in the morning, and offered burnt offerings according to the number of them all: for Job said, It may be that my sons have sinned, and cursed God in their hearts. Thus did Job continually. (Job 1:5)

And then shall many be offended, and shall betray one another, and shall hate one another. (Matthew 24:10)

And he said, A certain man had two sons: And the younger of them said to his father, Father, give me the portion of goods that falleth to me. And he divided unto them his living. And not many days after the younger son gathered all together, and took his journey into a far country, and there wasted his substance with riotous living. (Luke 15:11–13)

How think ye? if a man have an hundred sheep, and one of them be gone astray, doth he not leave the ninety and nine, and goeth into the mountains, and seeketh that which is gone astray? And if so be that he find it, verily I say unto you, he rejoiceth more of that sheep, than of the ninety and nine which went not astray. Even so it is not the will of your Father which is in heaven, that one of these little ones should perish. (Matthew 18:12–14)

And he spake this parable unto them, saying, What man of you, having an hundred sheep, if he lose one of them, doth not leave the ninety and nine in the wilderness, and go after that which is lost, until he find it? And when he hath found it, he layeth it on his shoulders. (Luke 15:3–5)

Be ye not unequally yoked together with unbelievers: for what fellowship hath righteousness with unrighteousness? and what communion hath light with darkness? And what concord hath Christ with Belial? or what part hath he that believeth with an infidel? (2 Corinthians 6:14–15)

I had fainted, unless I had believed to see the goodness of the Lord in the land of the living. (Psalm 27:13)

For I know the thoughts that I think toward you, saith the Lord, thoughts of peace, and not of evil, to give you an expected end. (Jeremiah 29:11)

Remember his marvellous works that he hath done, his wonders, and the judgments of his mouth. (1 Chronicles 16:12)

And thou shalt teach them diligently unto thy children, and shalt talk of them when thou sittest in thine house, and when thou walkest by the way, and when thou liest down, and when thou risest up. (Deuteronomy 6:7)

But other fell into good ground, and brought forth fruit, some an hundredfold, some sixtyfold, some thirtyfold. (Matthew 13:8)

And so he that had received five talents came and brought other five talents, saying, Lord, thou deliveredst unto me five talents: behold, I have gained beside them five talents more. His lord said unto him, Well done, thou good and faithful servant: thou hast been faithful over a few things, I will make thee ruler over many things: enter thou into the joy of thy lord. (Matthew 25:20–21)

But if any widow have children or nephews, let them learn first to shew piety at home, and to requite their parents: for that is good and acceptable before God. (1 Timothy 5:4)

As the Lord hath been with my lord the king, even so be he with Solomon, and make his throne greater than the throne of my lord king David. (1 Kings 1:37)

The secret things belong unto the Lord our God: but those things which are revealed belong unto us and to our children for ever, that we may do all the words of this law. (Deuteronomy 29:29)

Now the days of David drew nigh that he should die; and he charged Solomon his son, saying, I go the way of all the earth: be thou strong therefore, and shew thyself a man; And keep the charge of the Lord thy God, to walk in his ways, to keep his statutes, and his commandments, and his judgments, and his testimonies, as it is written in the law of Moses, that thou mayest prosper in all that thou doest, and whithersoever thou turnest thyself. (1 Kings 2:1–3)

Now there was no smith found throughout all the land of Israel: for the Philistines said, Lest the Hebrews make them swords or spears. (1 Samuel 13:19)

Train up a child in the way he should go: and when he is old, he will not depart from it. (Proverbs 22:6)

Foolishness is bound in the heart of a child; but the rod of correction shall drive it far from him. (Proverbs 22:15)

He that spareth his rod hateth his son: but he that loveth him chasteneth him betimes. (Proverbs 13:24)

He hath also prepared for him the instruments of death; he ordaineth his arrows against the persecutors. (Psalm 7:13)

Yea, he sent out his arrows, and scattered them; and he shot out lightnings, and discomfited them. (Psalm 18:14)

Make bright the arrows; gather the shields: the Lord hath raised up the spirit of the kings of the Medes: for his device is against Babylon, to destroy it; because it is the vengeance of the Lord, the vengeance of his temple. (Jeremiah 51:11)

And the Lord shall be seen over them, and his arrow shall go forth as the lightning: and the Lord God shall blow the trumpet, and shall go with whirlwinds of the south. (Zechariah 9:14)

Wilt thou set thine eyes upon that which is not? for riches certainly make themselves wings; they fly away as an eagle toward heaven. (Proverbs 23:5)

Woe unto him that striveth with his Maker! Let the potsherd strive with the potsherds of the earth. Shall the clay say to him that fashioneth it, What makest thou? or thy work, He hath no hands? (Isaiah 45:9)

Hath not the potter power over the clay, of the same lump to make one vessel unto honour, and another unto dishonour? (Romans 9:21)

Surely your turning of things upside down shall be esteemed as the potter's clay: for shall the work say of him that made it, He made me not? or shall the thing framed say of him that framed it, He had no understanding? (Isaiah 29:16)

Sharp arrows of the mighty, with coals of juniper. (Psalm 120:4)

And he hath made my mouth like a sharp sword; in the shadow of his hand hath he hid me, and made me a polished shaft; in his quiver hath he hid me. (Isaiah 49:2)

Ye are of God, little children, and have overcome them: because greater is he that is in you, than he that is in the world. (1 John 4:4)

And he answered, Fear not: for they that be with us are more than they that be with them. (2 Kings 6:16)

LABOR PAIN

And five of you shall chase an hundred, and an hundred of you shall put ten thousand to flight: and your enemies shall fall before you by the sword. (Leviticus 26:8)

How should one chase a thousand, and two put ten thousand to flight, except their Rock had sold them, and the Lord had shut them up? (Deuteronomy 32:3)

Again I say unto you, That if two of you shall agree on earth as touching any thing that they shall ask, it shall be done for them of my Father which is in heaven. For where two or three are gathered together in my name, there am I in the midst of them. (Matthew 18:19–20)

Two are better than one; because they have a good reward for their labour. For if they fall, the one will lift up his fellow: but woe to him that is alone when he falleth; for he hath not another to help him up. (Ecclesiastes 4:9–10)

And Jesus knew their thoughts, and said unto them, Every kingdom divided against itself is brought to desolation; and every city or house divided against itself shall not stand. (Matthew 12:25)

And if a house be divided against itself, that house cannot stand. (Mark 3:25)

Can two walk together, except they be agreed? (Amos 3:3)

Honor thy father and thy mother: that thy days may be long upon the land which the Lord thy God giveth thee. (Exodus 20:12)

Honor, thy father and thy mother, as the Lord thy God hath commanded thee; that thy days may be prolonged, and that it may go well with thee, in the land which the Lord thy God giveth thee. (Deuteronomy 5:16)

Honour thy father and mother; which is the first commandment with promise. (Ephesians 6:2)

And there was a widow in that city; and she came unto him, saying, Avenge me of mine adversary. And he would not for a while: but afterward he said within himself, Though I fear not God, nor regard man; Yet because this widow troubleth me, I will avenge her, lest by her continual coming she weary me. (Luke 18:3–5)

Let us therefore come boldly unto the throne of grace, that we may obtain mercy, and find grace to help in time of need. (Hebrews 4:16)

And all his sons and all his daughters rose up to comfort him; but he refused to be comforted; and he said, For I will go down into the grave unto my son mourning. Thus his father wept for him. (Genesis 37:35)

Then the word of the Lord came unto me, saying, Before I formed thee in the belly I knew thee; and before thou camest forth out of the womb I sanctified thee, and I ordained thee a prophet unto the nations. (Jeremiah 1:4–5)

For whom he did foreknow, he also did predestinate to be conformed to the image of his Son, that he might be the firstborn among many brethren. (Romans 8:29)

I will praise thee; for I am fearfully and wonderfully made: marvellous are thy works; and that my soul knoweth right well. (Psalm 139:14)

Therefore take no thought, saying, What shall we eat? or, What shall we drink? or, Wherewithal shall we be clothed? (Matthew 6:31)

But Jesus said, Suffer little children, and forbid them not, to come unto me: for of such is the kingdom of heaven. (Matthew 19:14)

But Jesus called them unto him, and said, Suffer little children to come unto me, and forbid them not: for of such is the kingdom of God. (Luke 18:16)

But if any provide not for his own, and specially for those of his own house, he hath denied the faith, and is worse than an infidel. (1 Timothy 5:8)

A good name is rather to be chosen than great riches, and loving favour rather than silver and gold. (Proverbs 22:1)

A good name is better than precious ointment; and the day of death than the day of one's birth. (Ecclesiastes 7:1)

Wherefore come out from among them, and be ye separate, saith the Lord, and touch not the unclean thing; and I will receive you. (2 Corinthians 6:17)

Listen as Wisdom calls out! Hear as understanding raises her voice! (Proverbs 8: 1–2)

For God hath not given us the spirit of fear; but of power, and of love, and of a sound mind. (2 Timothy 1:7)

But Jesus looked at them and said, "With man this is impossible." (Matthew 19:26)

In those days Hezekiah became ill and was at the point of death. The prophet Isaiah son of Amoz went to him and said, "This is what the Lord says: Put your house in order, because you are going to die; you will not recover."

Then the word of the Lord came to Isaiah: "Go and tell Hezekiah, 'This is what the Lord, the God of your father David, says: I have heard your prayer and seen your tears; I will add fifteen years to your life. (Isaiah 38:1,4–5)

Foolishness is bound in the heart of a child; but the rod of correction shall drive it far from him. (Proverbs 22:15)

THE SYMBOLISM OF THE GREEN ROSE

All roses symbolize God's love at work on earth, but the green rose is symbolic of mother earth, the greatest force, and the true essence of life. The myth about the green rose can be traced back to China in the 18th century. The tale had it that green roses were given in the legendary Forbidden City and belonging solely to the emperor. Later in 1856, the British nursery Bembridge and Harrison acquired some and then introduced them to the public. Because they were known for their big blooms, they became obsessed with the British that couldn't get enough of them. Although not as popular as the red roses, green roses have widely spread around the world and are a sight to behold, but the green roses are uniquely known for these:

Green Roses classic color represents prosperity, wealth, fertility, and abundance of everything

Green Roses significantly represent maternity, increase & wholeness in all aspects of life.

Green Roses are a symbol of flourishing growth, the richness of nature, and completeness of life

Green Roses symbolize the posterity, spirit & rejuvenation of life, and spirit found in nature

Green Roses are associated with serenity, richness in mind & spirit, and completeness.

Green Roses symbolizes balance, stability, a peaceful feeling, and harmony in life.

Green Roses are attuned with traits, thus a right gift for someone with a calm demeanor

A bright green rose is a perfect flower to show others you think positively about their future

A silent message to a loved one that you wish to have and enjoy the gift of children

And the best of all

Green Roses Depict Eternal Love

To Ody   ChiChi   Du

From google search

With my eternal love, Mom